Ashley Field and Irk Town

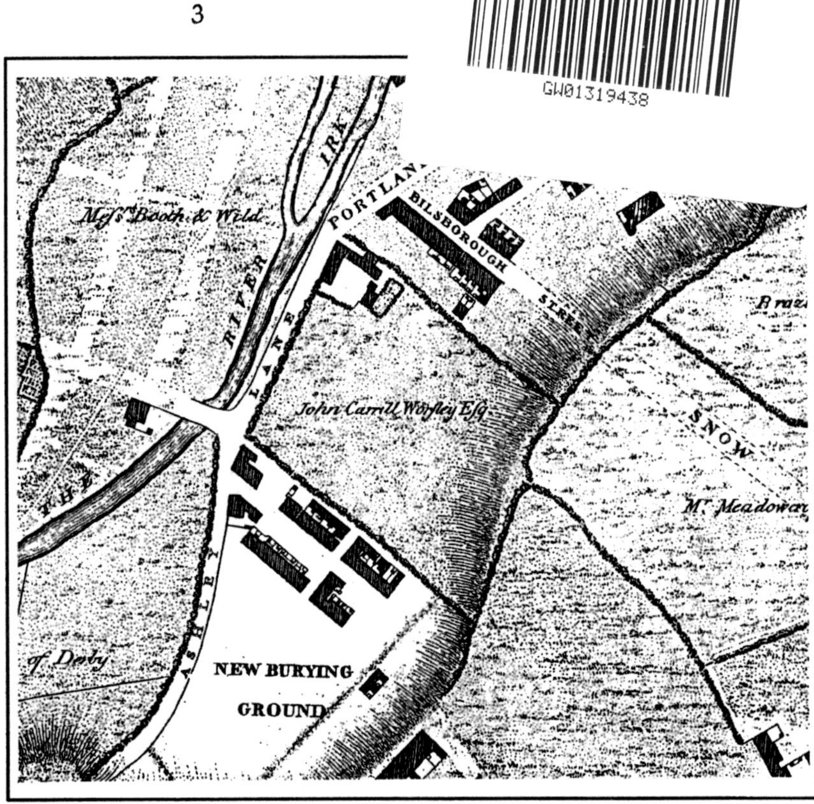

Green's 1794 map shows Ashley Field, the property of John Carrill Worsley, and the Irk valley on the eve of rapid industrial development.

In December 1982, in a neglected area of Collyhurst where the railway viaduct crosses the River Irk, passers-by saw a demolition contractor at work. The joiner's shop under demolition had an unusual distinction. Apparently one building, it was once fourteen back-to-back houses with two cellar dwellings. Over two hundred years ago the land upon which this building stood was called Ashley Field.

At the spot where Angel Street, Blakeley Street and Ashley Lane met, once stood a *'magnificent house and grounds from which one of the most beautiful views of vale and river, hill and woodland could be had'.*

Ashley Field would have been part of this beautiful view, yet in the late eighteenth century the rural nature of Ashley Field was already doomed. It was shortly to become a slum in a no-man's-land between Angel Meadow and Newtown. By 1762 the once clear, winding River Irk had, according to the 'General Magazine of Arts and Sciences', over 300 mills along its banks. There had been a paper mill near Smedley since at least 1730 and there was calico printing at Little Green Works by 1763. Green's map of 1794 shows a dyeworks near the Collyhurst Mills and others are situated along the river nearer to the town. Across the river in Red Bank is an iron foundry. Johnson's map of 1820

John Street in 1982, awaiting demolition. The frontage on Back Irk Street with the 'For Sale' sign is the same as that on the front cover.

shows that there had been a steady growth of industry and housing in Newtown and Red Bank in the intervening twenty-five years. Much of this newly developed land belonged to the Earl of Derby and further out towards Collyhurst the land was owned by the lord of the manor, Sir Oswald Mosley.

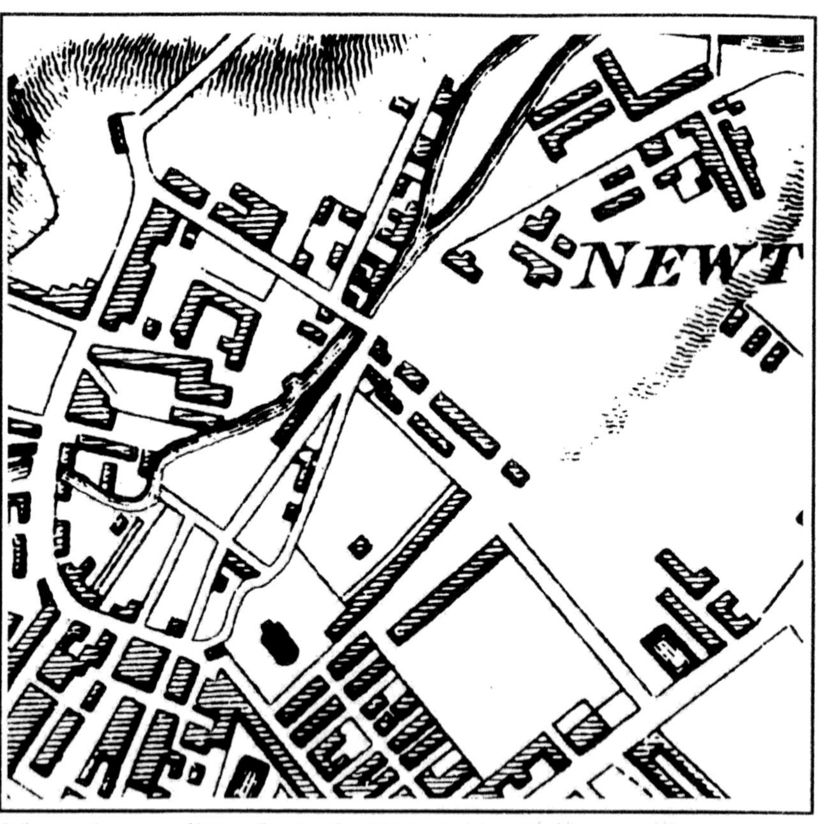

Johnson's map of Manchester in 1820. Ashley Field was still open.

To the south of the river, Brazennose College, Oxford, and the Collegiate Church were large landowners. Here and there, however, were isolated patches belonging to other people. Ashley Field was one of these. Sloping steeply down to the Irk west of the junction of Ashley Lane and Portland Street, it was owned in 1794 by John Carill Worsley of Platt Hall in Rusholme. The land had a recorded history dating to 1326 and had been in the Worsley family since at least 1587. In the sixteenth century the town swineherd passed Ashley Field daily as he took the town's pigs along the river to Collyhurst Common. A century later James Cheetham was ascribing *'the goodness and deliciousness'* of the eels taken from the Irk to the *'numerousness of fulling mills that stood upon that river'.* Another hundred years on, Green's map records the dyeworks and iron foundries which preceded the rapid industrial development of the early nineteenth century.

Late eighteenth century houses at the corner of Irk Street and Cross Irk Street. The upper storeys have workshops which could have been used by handloom weavers, bootmakers, cabinet makers or other domestic craftsmen.

Industrial development made cottage building a necessity and in 1795 the area around Ashley Field was already being used for this. Water Street and Irish Row had been built by the river and the houses to the east in Flag Row and Dixon Street had assessed annual rents of only £1.10.0d to £2.10.0d in 1795. To the west were Irk Street and the houses of well-to-do people in Old Mount Street. George Street, later known as Rochdale Road, and Gould Street were being built on to the south. Ashley Field itself was as yet untouched and increasing in value as buildings went up all around it in the next thirty years.

When development came in the 1820s it was rapid. This was the decade when Manchester's population increased by nearly fifty percent and new houses were urgently needed for the flood of immigrants. Bancks' map of 1831 has a very different picture from its predecessors. Ashley Field had been laid out in a grid of five streets running east to west from Bromley Street to Back Irk Street, and another four streets running north to south, from Ashley Lane to Charlotte Street. South of Charlotte Street, on land owned by Mr Fielding in 1794, now stood the town's No.2 Gas Works. In all, there were some 138 houses upon Ashley Field, built between the surveys of 1820 and 1831, and the area was now known as Irk Town.

Irk Town lay between Newtown and Angel Meadow, next to the New Parish Burial Ground which adjoined the graveyard of St Michael's Church, a carriage church built in 1789. Employment was to be found by 1828 in Parker's Mill and education and spiritual guidance were provided by Ashley Lane Sunday School, built in 1827. Six dwellings had been built on the east side of Back Irk Street between 1820 and 1824, two with cellar dwellings below, facing Back Irk Street, and two built back-to-back with them facing what was to become Silver Street.

Three two-up-two-downs with cellar dwellings were built on the south side of John Street between 1826 and 1827. The following decade saw the infilling of the remaining spaces. Ten back-to-back houses completed the north side of John Street and Back Ashley Lane in 1836-37 and the two remaining gaps were filled in 1843 and 1844.

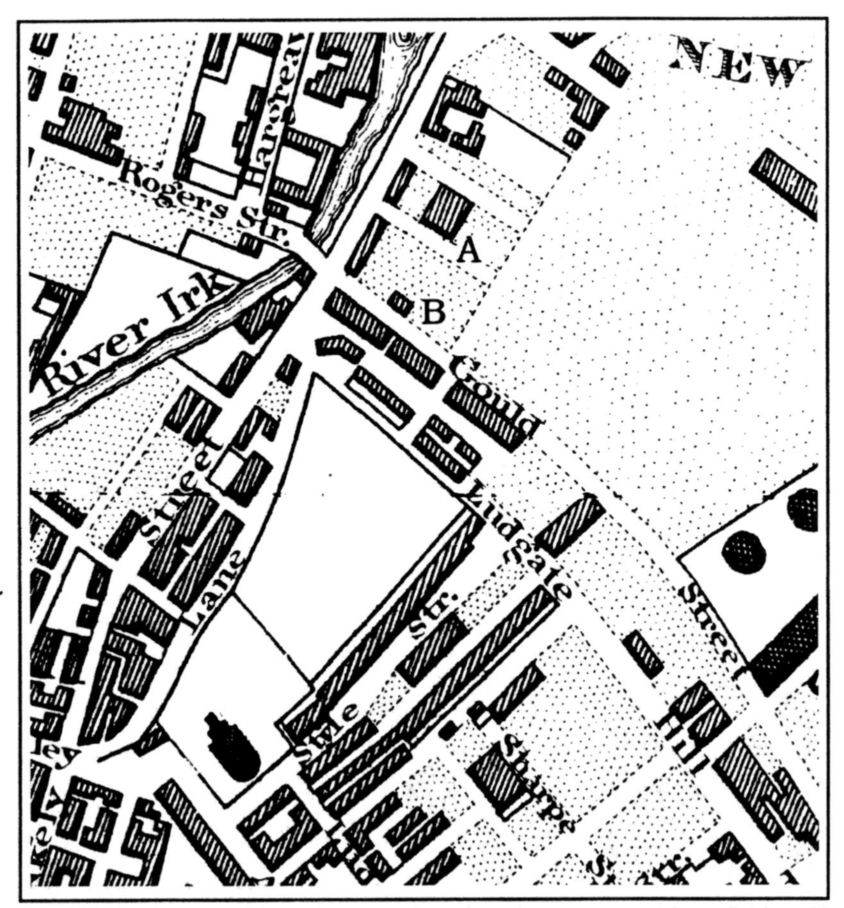

Baines' map of 1824 shows the first buildings on Ashley Field, with shops and houses along Ashley Lane, Parker Street Mill (A) and the first of the John Street houses (B), two with cellar dwellings facing Gould Street (later Back Irk Street) and their two back houses facing the mill.

By 1850 only one space on the south side of Charlotte Street remained, and that had still not been built upon by 1911.

The final influence upon the topography of Ashley Field was the Manchester and Leeds Railway. The extension of the line from Oldham Road to Hunts Bank in 1842 involved some demolition. The old boundaries of Ashley Field defined the census enumeration districts in 1841 and 1851 and the numbers of houses recorded in the district in those years declined from 156 to 135, a decrease of 21 at a time when more, not fewer, houses were needed. Further demolition took place after 1890 when the Lancashire and Yorkshire Railway widened the viaduct.

Between 1830 and 1930 Irk Town was subject to inspection by some of the most perceptive and critical observers of industrial Manchester. Their descriptions of the area give a horrific picture of what it was like to live there.

In 1831 British doctors prepared themselves for the inevitable onslaught of the frightening new disease spreading across Europe - cholera. Experience of fever in Manchester and cholera on the Continent suggested the areas and the people who were most likely to suffer from the dreaded disease. The poor in their overcrowded and insanitary dwellings, with insufficient water and privies, and with defective or inadequate drainage, would suffer most. Dr Kay, the physician at Ancoats Dispensary, and a member of Manchester's Board of Health, began an inspection of those parts of the town where the poor lived. He referred particularly *'to Back Irk Street, and to the state of almost the whole of that mass of cottages filling the insalubrious valley through which the Irk flows,'* and to the Irk, which *'receives excrementitious matter from some sewers in this portion of the town - the drainage from the Gas Works, and filth of the most pernicious character from bone works, tanneries, size manufactories &c.'*

People who lived in the low-lying parts of the town and in the river valleys were particularly vulnerable to the filth which washed down from above, and Irk Town was no exception. Another of the observers at this time was Dr Henry Gaulter, who determined to investigate the cause of cholera. To this end he set himself the task of following up the circumstances of the first 200 victims in Manchester. Back Irk Street had nine cases, amongst whom were the Hannah sisters. Concerning their case, Gaulter noted *'that the common sewer which holds a subterranean course till it gets opposite the door where they lived, escapes by a large aperture of masonry just at that point, and then continues to flow above ground to the bottom of the street when it enters the Irk.'*

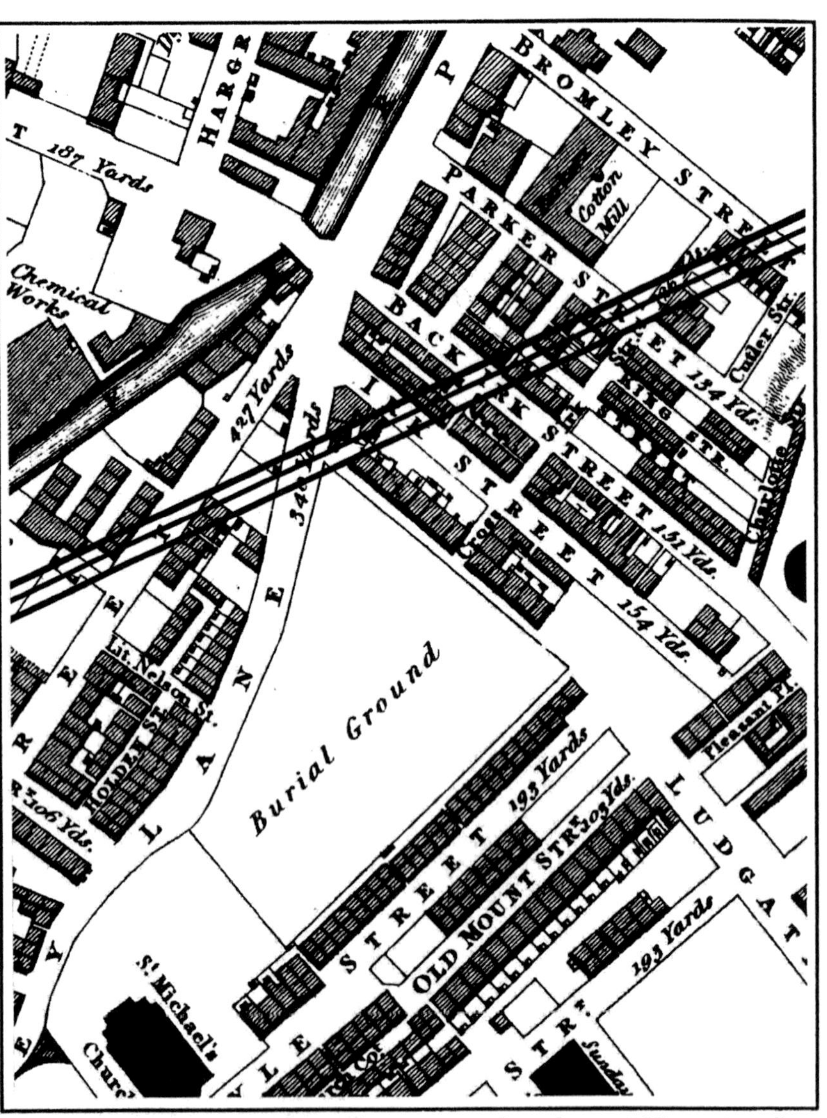

The Manchester & Leeds Railway extension from Oldham Road to Hunts Bank caused the demolition of twenty-one much-needed houses on Ashley Field alone. The line of the intended railway is here drawn on Banks's 1831 plan, to which have also been added the John Street houses built between 1831 and 1839.

The sewer flowed past the doors and cellar entrances of 46 and 48 Back Irk Street. The remaining ten cottages on John Street and Back Ashley Lane were still to be built in 1832 and this random development was noticed by the most famous visitor who could ever have walked along John Street, Frederick Engels.

By 1844, when Engels came down the Irk valley from Old Town, he described a place where *'all the features of a city are lost. Single rows of houses or groups of streets stand here and there, like little villages on the naked, not even grass-grown clay soil; the houses, or rather cottages, are in bad order, never repaired, filthy, with damp unclean cellar dwellings; the lanes are neither paved, nor supplied with sewers, but harbour numerous colonies of swine penned in small sties or yards, or wandering unrestrained through the neighbourhood.'*

An observer with a different attitude, Angus Bethune Reach, found in Manchester in 1849 *'an evident disposition to improvement'* but not in Angel Meadow, *'the lowest, most filthy, most unhealthy and most wicked locality in Manchester.'* Reach saved his most graphic description for the part of Angel Meadow nearer to Irk Town. In the 'Dog and Duck' in Charter Street, *'a haunt of the superior class of prigs'* (thieves) he saw prostitutes who *'had formerly held a higher position in their wretched class'* and a number of bare-footed boys drinking there, many of whom were pickpockets. These people were well off compared with those in the nearby lodging in a cellar, *'the worst in all Manchester'*, who shared indescribable conditions with a half grown calf and an old man who slept in a hole dug through the foundations, six foot long, two feet deep and about a foot high, who *'would have to sleep in the streets'* had not the landlady extended him this charity.

In 1849 cholera returned to

Manchester, and Leigh and Gardiner's contemporary map shows Irk Town to have been severely affected. Their history of the outbreak mentioned that the streets there had been recently and excellently paved and sewered and were regularly swept, yet the houses, having been built before this was done, were badly drained, ill-ventilated and lacking in water. Cases of cholera were recorded in Parker Street, Charter Street, St Michael's Place and Flag Alley between June and October and ninety-four cases had been recorded in Angel Meadow by the end of September.

Cock fighting was one of the amusements to be seen on the Parish Burial Ground adjoining St Michael's Churchyard. This fight took place in Moston in the 1820s.

A further outbreak in 1853 led to the formation of the Manchester and Salford Sanitary Association. The Rochdale Road Committee of the Association included the vicar of St Michael's and Mr Holcroft of Parker Street Mill, and they inspected their district between 1853 and 1854. In the immediate vicinity of John Street, the condition of the parish burial ground, closed in 1816 after only twenty-nine years, gave cause for concern. Burials in 1816 had taken place in pits rather than in single graves, an *'expeditious and economical'* method thoroughly

Back Irk Street in September 1909. Nos.46 and 48 are on the left. Twenty-two people, of whom fourteen were weavers, lived in these two houses in 1841.

approved of by contemporary writer Joseph Aston. At the time of its closure more than 40,000 dead rested there, but not in peace. The old burial ground was the only open space in Angel Meadow and the turbulent inhabitants did not want to waste it; it was a cock pit, a tip, a prize-fighters' ring, a gambling den and served other more profitable purposes. Writing in 1899, Arthur G Symonds remembered that *'barrowfuls of human bones used to be dug up and taken away and sold for a few coppers, to be ground up and used for bone dust, manure, and according to popular tradition, for flour.'*

The Rochdale Road Committee recommended that *'some immediate steps should be taken to remove what is evidently most detrimental to the health as well as the morals of the people.'*

In the following decade the condition of the burial ground had become such a scandal that there was a public enquiry and it was closed in 1868. The rector of St Michael's started a campaign to have the area converted to a children's playground, a campaign eventually crowned with success. By 1892 a Ragged School teacher wrote in the 'Manchester City News' of the *'Flags with its garden patches, its large playgrounds and its swings and gymnasium* (which) *must improve the physique of the children in every way.'*

St Michael's Church, built for well-to-do people in 1789, was surrounded by slums by 1830 and was demolished in the 1930s.

Muscular Christianity did what it could but the Rev. Mercer, in his paper 'The Condition of Life in Angel Meadow' presented to the Manchester Statistical Society on April 28th, 1897, described conditions which would have been familiar to Kay, Gaulter and Engels; of insanitary and overcrowded dwellings, chronic ill health and high mortality, drunkenness, prostitution and pauperism.

The area was beyond redemption; the closing two decades of the nineteenth century saw reconditioning of old properties, the replacement of midden privies, first with pail privies and then with water closets, but the only answer to the insoluble problems of the area lay in demolition or the closure of the dwellings as unfit for human habitation.

Some of the dwellings thus closed entered upon a new life as commercial premises, a practice which did not make the area better to live in for those who remained. One new industry introduced at this time was the making of waterproof cloth, which added the smell of rubber to air which had not grown sweeter during the century.

The opening descriptions of Irk Town concerned the Irk itself. It may be appropriate to leave the last word to the committee of the Manchester and Salford Better Housing Council which reported in 1931 that *'the Irk itself is rich in colour and is perfumed from the factories which lie further up its banks. On a hot summer's day existence in the houses nearest it must be almost intolerable.'*

John Street

The Building of John Street

A careful study of maps and rate books between 1820 and 1830 reveals the first cottage building in Ashley Field and John Street. Baines' Manchester Directory of 1825 does not include John Street in his complete list of streets and courts but his contemporary map, surveyed in 1824, shows the first six dwellings: four cottages built back-to-back behind Ashley Lane, the two facing Back Irk Street with cellar dwellings.

The 1825 rate book indicates a flurry of cottage building, with cottages described as 'new' between Back Irk Street and Parker Street, and by 1827 it is possible to identify three cottages with rateable values of £5.5.0d, which by 1828 were described as being in John Street. In 1839, when the Manchester and Leeds Railway Company was planning an extension from Oldham Road to Hunts Bank, Stephenson, Gooch and Johnson surveyed the proposed line, and a list of the properties, with descriptions and the names of their landowners, landlords and tenants, was provided in the accompanying 'Book of Reference'. It shows that the land on which these three cottages stood was the only part of Ashley Field no longer in the possession of Thomas Carill Worsley. The land belonged to four men; Samuel Thorpe, a beer retailer with premises on the corner of Ashley Lane and Back Irk Street, and the three trustees of the Griffin Building Club: Samuel Cheetham, licensee of the Heywood Arms on Oldham Road, George Innes junior, a letterpress printer of Back Turner Street, and George Perkins. The three cottages had cellar dwellings and were two storeys high with four rooms. They always had a higher rateable value than the back-to-backs opposite them across John Street, which were two-roomed houses. In 1827 the landlord of the three cottages was Henry Lees, an earthenware dealer from Bank Top.

The rest of Ashley Field remained in the hands of Mr Carill Worsley and various business associates. He owned Silver Street, which connected John Street to Charlotte Street, jointly with Mr Charles Pilling, another Rusholme gentleman. The one-up-one-down back-to-back cottages had a rateable value in 1839 of £3.5.0d, by which time the houses built by the Griffin Building Club were rated at £4.15.0d. The higher rateable value of the Griffin houses was maintained until their closure in or after 1888, with the middle one sometimes having a slightly higher rating of £6.10.0d compared with £6.0.0d for the two on either side in 1880. This middle house was sometimes a shop and may have been slightly superior to the other two.

By 1832 only two areas of Ashley Field remained open. The first was the south-east corner opposite the Gas Works, built in 1824. This land had still not been built on by 1911 and would almost certainly have contained a great amount of refuse throughout most of the nineteenth century. The only other open patch was the area between Silver Street and Parker Street, facing the Griffin houses. In 1836 the houses at

No.7 John Street in 1982. The height of the door was only five feet six inches. There were two steps down into the ground floor room.

the back of 46 and 48 Back Irk Street were empty; they were presumably being altered, since the 1837 rate books listed ten new houses adjoining them, built over Silver Street which now finished on the south side of John Street. The new houses were back-to-back, consisting of four facing the Griffin houses, with a John Street address, two facing Parker Street, and four facing the backs of houses on Ashley Lane. A wall separated the new houses from these and the address of the four facing this wall was Back Ashley Lane. The 'lane' was at one end a mere four feet wide and ten feet wide at the other end, as is clearly seen in the maps, and John Street was about eighteen feet wide. The new houses did not have cellars and the two older houses backing on to 46 and 48 Back Irk Street had been altered so that their doors now opened on to John Street and Back Ashley Lane.

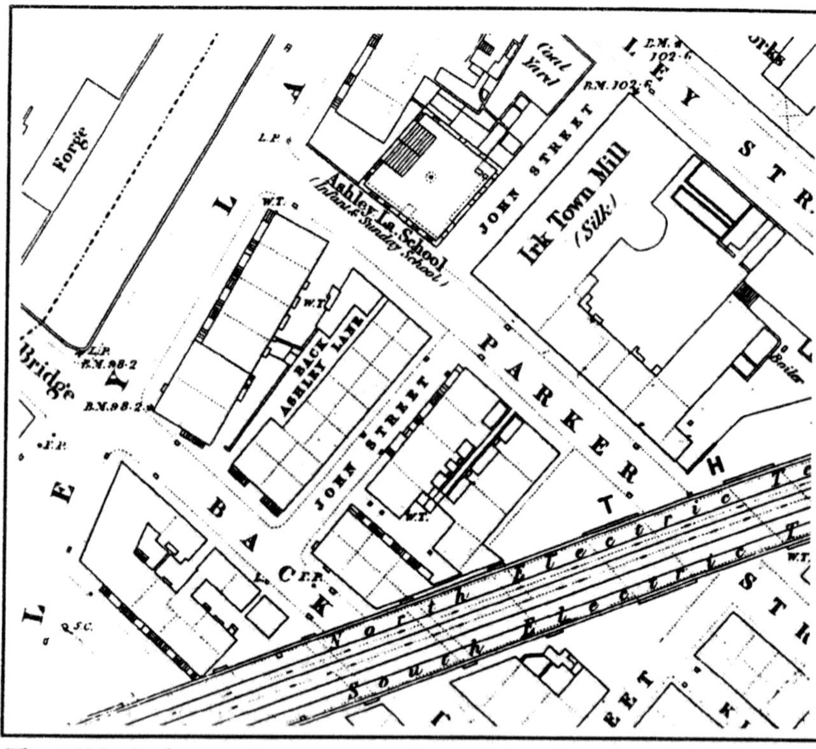

The 1850 Ordnance Survey map shows John Street as the inspectors from the Manchester and Salford Sanitary Association saw it.

The 'Book of Reference' accompanying the Manchester and Leeds Railway extension survey of 1839 describes the Back Ashley Lane cottages as having outbuildings and these can be seen on the 1850 Ordnance Survey map. The same survey shows that houses facing 46 and 48 Back Irk Street had pig cotes between that street and Irk Street, confirming Engels' observation referred to on page six. The inhabitants of the new houses were certainly familiar with pigs, even if they did not keep them themselves.

The Rochdale Road Committee of the Manchester and Salford Sanitary Association commented that John Street and Back Ashley Lane were deficient in *'petty accommodation'* and there do not seem to have been more than two outbuildings marked on the 1850 Ordnance Survey map which could have been privies. There was a water tap at the back of Ashley Lane, on the other side of the wall facing 2 to 10 Back Ashley Lane, and another behind 2 John Street in Silver Court (created when the railway extension cut off and left stranded a small number of

The unplanned nature of early nineteenth century development can be seen on this photograph taken in 1899 from under the railway bridge over Irk Street. It shows the corner shop between Ashley Lane and Charter Street (left), houses on Ashley Lane built before 1820, and the iron foundry on Red Bank across the river.

houses which had once been part of Silver Street).

2 John Street was the last house to be built on that side in 1839, filling in a space previously used as a coal yard. In 1843-44, at the side of 25 Parker Street, the last space was filled in with 27 Parker Street. From then onwards, Back Ashley Lane was entered by a tunnel.

It is not too difficult to establish the chronology of building and tenancy from maps and rate books, but there are some problems in relying on rate books. One is the sudden recording of cellar tenants from 1852. There was no earlier reference in the rate books to the use of cellars as dwellings, but the Manchester and Leeds Railway Survey of 1839 gave the names of all the tenants in John Street and included those of the five who lived in the cellars. Their recording in the rate books after 1852 indicated a new policy, not a new way of using the cellars.

Another complication arises between 1852 and 1853, when all the tenants appear to have moved house. However, a closer examination shows that the houses had been renumbered. The Manchester Police Act of 1830 had required that all streets be renumbered odd on one side and even on the other, but this was not effected in John Street until 1853. The numbering of John Street varied at different times, partly because of the haphazard way in which it had developed, and this is illustrated on the plans shown here. The only way to ascertain certain identification of individual houses is to make a tenancy record for each one, and the average recorded tenancy is about two years!

No.4 Back Ashley Lane in 1982. The projecting part, with a new external wall, is two of the four houses built on Back Irk Street before 1824. Patrick Flaherty moved into No.4 after the closure of his cellar dwelling in 1872.

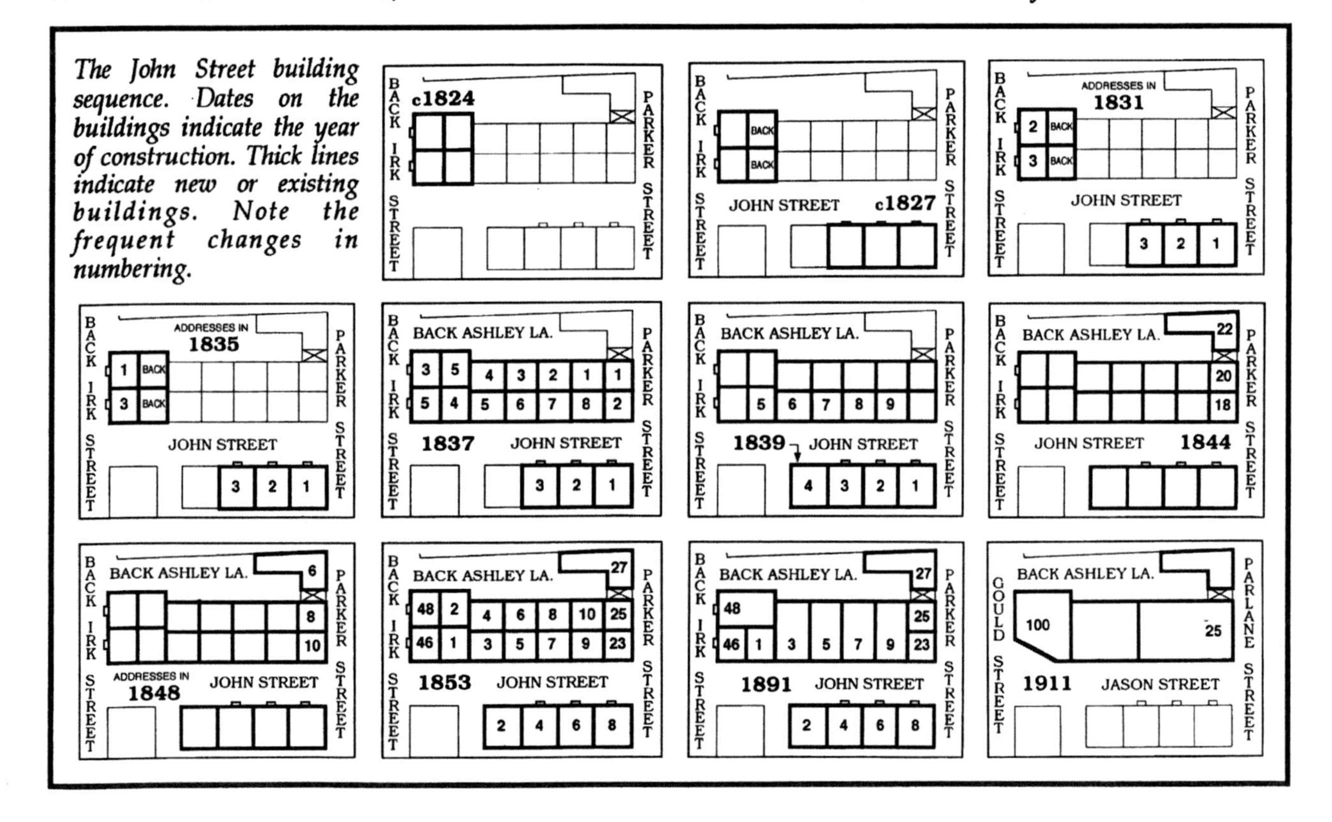

The John Street building sequence. Dates on the buildings indicate the year of construction. Thick lines indicate new or existing buildings. Note the frequent changes in numbering.

John Street

John Street and the Sanitary Movement

The growth of the sanitary movement in the 1840s directed the attention of such groups as the Manchester Statistical Society, the Manchester and Salford Sanitary Association and the Education Aid Society to the urgent sanitary and social problems of such areas as Irk Town. During the next two decades, social and sanitary reformers and philanthropists responded by introducing Ragged Schools, extending Day and Sunday School provision and by giving public health lectures in St Michael's School at night. In 1853 a Ragged School was begun in Miller Street, which moved to Sharp Street the next year; Angel Meadow (later to become Charter Street) Ragged School, was opened in 1861 and Ashley Lane Sunday School's single storey of 1827 had been extended by two more storeys in 1844.

The City Council responded rather more slowly. Until the appointment of John Leigh in 1868 as Medical Officer of Health (late enough to scandalise the Social Science Association which held its annual meeting in Manchester in 1867) the work of M.O.H. was to some extent performed by the Manchester and Salford Sanitary Association. The scale of Leigh's problem was so great that he chose to tackle Manchester's exceedingly high mortality figures by an attack on midden privies and cesspools. Their replacement with pail privies took him ten years. During this time he also turned his attention to unsuitable and insanitary dwellings. Under the Manchester Corporation New Streets Act of 1853 he had powers to close cellar dwellings. The House Owners' Guardian Association had prevented the closing of many and only 176 were closed in the first six years following the Act. By 1872 Leigh had closed all but about 100. Among the last to be emptied were the five on John Street and Back Irk Street, which were recorded as occupied in the rate book of 1872, but never thereafter.

The greater problem of sub-standard and back-to-back housing he decided to tackle occasionally by demolition, but mainly by a policy of improvement which came to be known as reconditioning. This was to be carried out at the expense of the landlord and John Street was affected three times.

In 1888 the three Griffin houses, 4 to 8 John Street, were emptied, with only the newer 2 John Street remaining occupied. The proposed widening of the Lancashire and Yorkshire Railway may have been responsible for the closure; alternatively the Unhealthy Dwellings Sub-Committee of the Sanitary Committee may have condemned the houses. The chance survival of two records of the Unhealthy Dwellings Committee has preserved three items of relevance to John Street. One is a letter of March 25th 1890 in which the City Surveyor reported that the Lancashire and Yorkshire Railway Company was seeking powers for the widening of their line from Victoria to Oldham Road Station. The City Surveyor recommended that, *'wherever the Company cut through property they should be called upon to leave a 10 yards street in front of their viaduct; and wherever the ends of property abut upon this line, a passage at least 4 yards wide should be left.'*

This may throw light on the peculiar alteration which was made to 46 Back Irk Street and 1 John Street, and which is clearly shown on the Ordnance Survey

July 1898. Nos.4 to 8 John Street, built in 1826 by the Griffin Building Club as two up, two down houses with cellar dwellings. No.2 was built thirteen years later. The straight joint and different style can be seen very clearly. Parker's mill towers over the street. No.8, on the corner, housed nineteen people in 1871.

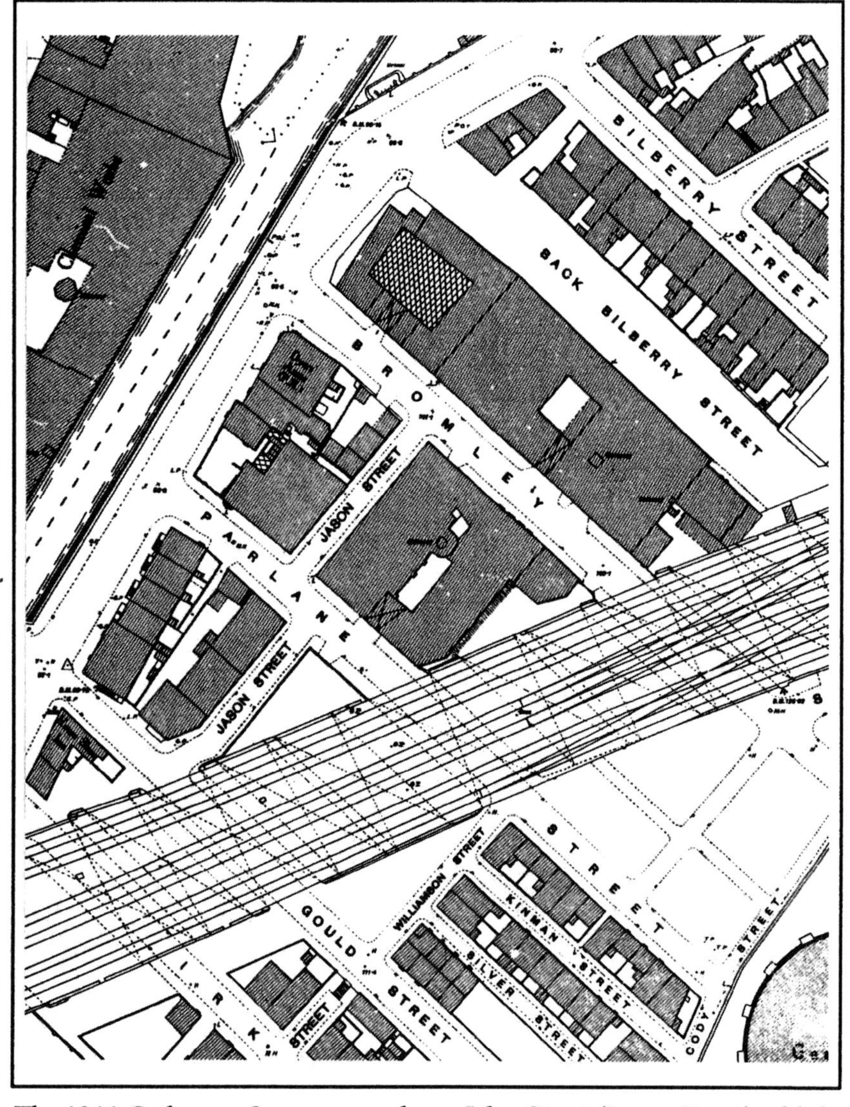

The 1911 Ordnance Survey map shows John Street (Jason Street) with its cut-off corner (see photo below), a consequence of the widening of the railway viaduct. At this time the property was being used as a mission.

map of 1911. The space between the houses and the viaduct would be less than thirteen feet, had the houses not been altered. After the alteration it was eighteen feet and two inches, and so conformed to the City Surveyor's recommendations.

Another letter illustrates the new policy introduced by Dr Tatham, Leigh's successor, *'that the Health Committee, the Paving, Sewering and Highways Committee and the Unhealthy Dwellings Committee be recommended to discourage the construction of pail closets in all new buildings and to sanction and encourage water closets instead.'*

Where reconditioning of insanitary dwellings took place, draining and sewering were also undertaken and water closets installed.

The only one of these documents to refer to John Street is reproduced on page 14, and indicates reconditioning in progress. 1890 was Back Ashley Lane's last year of separate existence; it was knocked through into John Street. The estimated weekly rental of the back-to-back cottages had been 2/9d but from 1891, for the through houses, it was 4/-. The landlords, Mr Evans and Miss Siddy, therefore had the expense of reconditioning and also suffered a reduction in the number of their properties and thus in their rents.

It took a keen eye to detect the blocked-up doorway and brick-arch lintels of the cellar windows on Gould Street in 1982. The smaller houses built in the 1830s extend up John Street on the right.

By the turn of the century 2 to 8 John Street had been pulled down for the widening of the railway line and the inhabited history of the former back-to-backs was drawing to a close. Still occupied in 1902, the houses were empty the following year and the rate book contains a note that they had been condemned on 3rd January 1903. Seventy-five years of occupation in John Street had come to an end.

1903 did not, however, mark the end of the useful life of the buildings and they had a curious history over the next thirty years. The original block of 1824, altered to suit the convenience of the Lancashire and Yorkshire Railway Company, was renumbered 100 Gould Street and became the Deutsche Gemeinde Mission. The remaining buildings, once back-to-back houses, were knocked into two separate premises, renumbered 25 Parker Street and let as workshops to Carl Scher and Joseph Samuels.

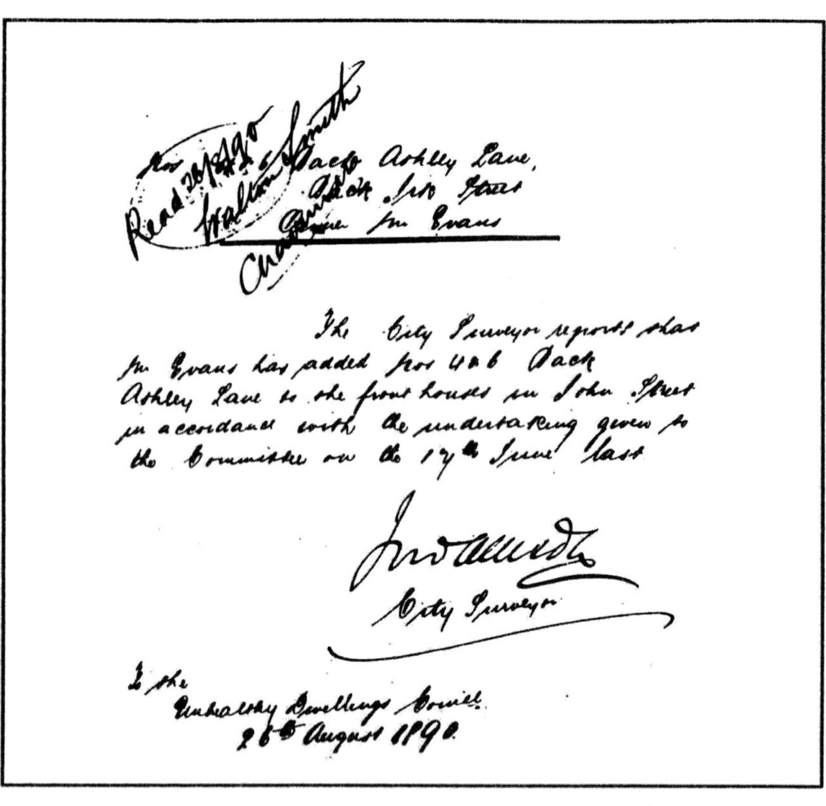

Read 26/8/1890 Walton Smith Chairman

Nos 4 & 6 Back Ashley Lane,
John Street
Owner Mr Evans

The City Surveyor reports that Mr Evans has added Nos 4 & 6 Back Ashley Lane to the front houses in John Street in accordance with the undertaking given to the Committee on the 17th June last

City Surveyor

To the Unhealthy Dwellings Committee.
26th August 1890.

Reconditioning in progress. Nos.4 and 6 Back Ashley Lane were knocked into 3 and 5 John Street to make 'through' houses in 1890.

Parker Street was renamed Parlane Street in 1910 and the workshop facing it was let to Albert Sharrocks as a works. The middle workshop was let to the mission as a club room. A mission with a German name had a short life expectancy by 1910 and the outbreak of war seemed to bring a great deal of activity to the area. The mission rooms were combined with 25 Parlane Street and let to the Standard Engineering Works by 1916.

The site of Nos.2 to 8 John Street in 1982. The houses were pulled down for the widening of the railway viaduct.

Mark Fink, a slipper manufacturer, first rented the entire block from Miss Siddy in 1921 for £58 a year. By 1926 Miss Siddy had sold 100 Gould Street to Mark Fink and the business was being run by Neville Joseph Fink. The Parlane Street end was let separately to Phillips & Co for £34. After 1931 the Parlane Waterproof Company Ltd occupied 100 Gould Street.

Five years later the Parlane Street end of the Finks' block was let as a joiner's shop and the other end was still tenanted by the Parlane Waterproof Company. The joinery business expanded into the rest of the building and it was used as a joiner's shop until Lady Day, 1982, when it became empty for the first time since the mid-1820s. It was still in the possession of Mark Fink's heirs when it was demolished in December 1982.

John Street

The Landlords

The ownership of the buildings changed frequently between 1824 and 1921. In John Street's twenty-three dwellings, for example, there was a total of eight different landlords over the twelve year period 1855-67, often as many as six at the same time. In the early 1840s the block of back-to-backs belonged to one local property owner, Samuel Thorpe, the beer retailer; 4 to 8 John Street, originally in the hands of Henry Lees of Bank Top, passed briefly to J J Parker in about 1831, back to Henry Lees, and then in 1842 to William Yates, later of Percival, Yates and Vickers, glass manufacturers of Collyhurst, until 1848. They were then sold to Thomas Vickers of the same firm and he continued to own them until the year before their closure in 1888.

After Samuel Thorpe's death in 1843, the back-to-back houses remained in the hands of various members of the Thorpe family until the last pair was sold to Eleazar Siddy in 1859. Siddy owned the bakery and grocer's shop next to Thorpe's beer shop on Ashley Lane. He had built 27 Parker Street in 1844, filling in the last space on the John Street site. He sold this to the Thorpes in 1847 and bought 46 and 48 Back Irk Street from them. Indeed, there were only nine years between 1844 and 1926 when a Siddy did not have an interest in these properties - from 1851 to 1860.

With very few exceptions John Street's landlords were local small traders and artisans. The rate books give only their names and, rarely, their addresses, but it is possible to discover their trades by using directories. From 1852 to 1867 James Galloway owned 7 and 9 John Street and 8 and 10 Back Ashley Lane. The only other Galloways in the directories at this time are the Galloways of Knott Mill Iron Foundry. In 1841 an iron moulder called James Galloway was living at 40 Ashley Lane, next to the Thorpes, and was still there in 1848. Since the large and long-established foundry which gave its name to Foundry Street on Red Bank was only just across the river, it seems likely that there was a connection between James and the Knott Mill Galloways.

In 1855 Joseph Stafford, the licensee of the Dyers Arms a little further along Ashley Lane, bought 23 to 27 Parker Street, then in 1865 he purchased 10 and 8 Back Ashley Lane from James Galloway and 2 Back Ashley Lane from Eleazar

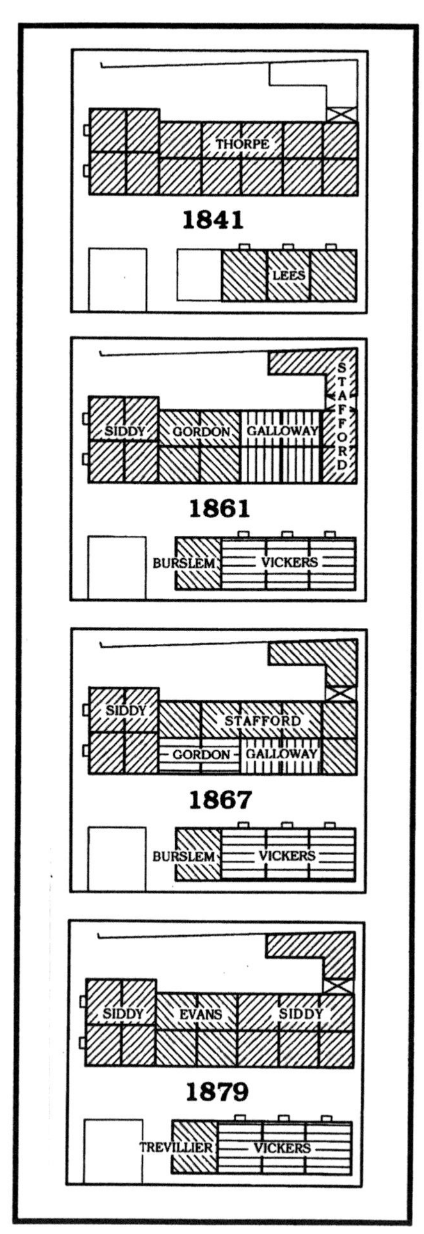

Examples of changes in landlords. Front and back houses were always owned by the same landlord except for the brief period when John Stafford owned Nos.4 to 10 Back Ashley lane and 23 to 27 Parker Street in 1867.

The Dyers Arms. There were dyeworks along the river and many of John Street's tenants were dyers.

Siddy. By 1867 he owned the whole of Back Ashley Lane, only to sell it again in 1869 to Eleazar Siddy and Henry Evans.

The period when Joseph Stafford owned Back Ashley Lane is a unique exception to the ownership pattern revealed by a detailed examination of the ownership of individual cottages. Although the addresses are quite different, the front and their corresponding back houses were always owned by the same person. So the properties which eventually became through houses had always had the same owner.

Henry Evans was also one of the humbler landlords, conspicuous only for the length of time that he owned his John Street property - from 1869 to 1895. Described as a labourer in a directory of 1871 and as a pointsman in 1876, he lived first in Bromley Street and then in Abercrombie Street. Other lesser landlords were Henry Read, a dyer of London Road in the 1830s, John Gordon, a painter and decorator of Blossom Street, and Thomas Rose, a joiner of Parker Street, in the 1850s.

At least three of John Street's landlords were men of substance and two of them were able to move right away from the area. Samuel Thorpe, the earliest of the three, was the first owner of 46 and 48 Back Irk Street with their back houses. Indeed, he may well have built the back-to-back houses on to them and was also the co-owner of the land beneath the Griffin houses. After his death in 1843 his widow continued to run the beer shop and his son Thomas inherited the property. Various other members of the family owned individual properties, selling the middle eight in 1851, 23 and 25 Parker Street in 1854, and 46 and 48 Back Irk Street in 1859.

John Jepson Parker is an example of a man of energy and drive who did very well for himself. Directories show his rise; the first reference to him is in 1824 when he is described as a reed manufacturer of Oak Street. By 1828 he was a reed manufacturer of Union Mills, Parker Street; his mills were attacked by a hungry mob the next year following a wage reduction, and 400 looms were destroyed. This may have influenced his next venture; in 1829 he was listed as 'spinner and manufacturer by power

The junction of Charter Street and Ashley Lane in 1907. The shop on the corner was once Siddy's bakery. John Street was behind this block.

and reed maker' of Middleton Court, Chapel Street in Salford. By 1832 he had three works, at Parker Street, Chapel Street and 1 York Street, Ducie Bridge. His trade was that of 'percher and stiffener' by 1836 and his Parker Street Mill was sold before 1843 to Richard Rothwell, who converted it to a silk mill. In 1845, his connection severed with Parker Street (which bore his name until 1910), he was described as a 'sizer and stiffener, wire drawer and pin manufacturer' of 3 York Street, with his house and another works at Adelphi Street, Salford.

Eleazar Siddy was the landlord with the longest connection with the Ashley Lane district. A successful businessman, his link with the John Street properties lasted from 1844 to his death in 1885 or 1886. He is first listed in the directories as a shopkeeper and baker of 15 Portland Street. By 1838 he was a baker, shopkeeper and flour dealer of 35 Ashley Lane. The Manchester and Leeds Railway extension survey of 1839 listed him as owning land and property between the New Burial Ground and Irk Street which included a house, shop, bakehouse and yard. It was a fairly extensive property and when it was demolished to make way for the railway he was able to obtain a better position for his new business, actually on Ashley Lane, next to Thorpe's beer shop. The 1841 census returns show him to have been a married man of about 38. He had no children but his establishment included an apprentice and a female servant. The address of his premises was 36 Ashley Lane in 1839, 35 in 1841 and 44 and 46 in 1843, by which time he had extended into the adjoining property. He bought some of the back houses on the block about that date and in 1844 built 27 Parker Street. The 1851 census shows his social advancement during the previous ten years. He was at the head of an establishment of three shopmen, one of whom eventually became the manager of the Ashley Lane business, a cook and a housemaid. He was 48 and his wife Mary Ann was 46; they were still childless. He bought and sold property in the area over the next few years but always kept some on the John Street block as well as the original grocery on Portland Street. By 1863 he had retired and moved away from Irk Town to an elegant new house, Cringlewood, in the pleasant suburb of Burnage. By now he had a new wife, who presented him with four daughters in rapid succession throughout his sixties. One of these, Annie, was to inherit his Irk Town property, although she herself spent the later part of her life in Blackpool. When the houses were condemned she bought out Henry Evans and let the property for other uses. Eleazar's investment in Newtown and Irk Town enabled him to retire to a very exclusive area with other rich and successful neighbours.

John Street seen from the Parker Street bridge in 1982. The houses and shops on Ashley Lane are a pile of rubble. The two houses facing Parker Street were Nos.23 and 25.

In the later nineteenth century Newtown and Irk Town experienced a second wave of immigrants. The Irish of the first wave had been partly dispersed by reconditioning and slum clearance, but Jews from Eastern Europe poured into the Irk valley late in the century. Mark Fink was one of these, the slipper manufacturer who in 1921 first rented and later bought the property then known as 100 Gould Street from Miss Siddy. It remained in the possession of his grandsons, Cecil and Geoffrey Fink, until 1982.

The ownership pattern of the twenty-three dwellings over this period makes it fairly clear that for most of the owners, possession was an investment. Many of them were local and at least three were men on their way up the social ladder. Maybe only Henry Evans, the 'labourer' and 'pointsman', obtained an essential income from them.

Life in Irk Town

The Records

At the Ashley Lane Sunday School Teachers' meeting on March 8th 1847, a letter of resignation from William Hadfield, the teacher of the third class, was read. William appealed to his colleagues not to lose heart at their apparent lack of success in bringing their pupils to the Lord. He reassured them that other teachers would continue the work *'when we shall be numbered with the forgotten generations.'*

William was right; the Ashley Lane Sunday School, a mission of the town centre society church, Grosvenor Street Chapel, served Irk Town from 1823 to 1936 and William himself was one of its successes. He had been associated with the school as pupil, monitor, secretary and teacher from 1826, the year when 4 to 8 John Street were first occupied. He and his fellow teachers must have known the inhabitants of the twenty-three dwellings well; 23 to 27 Parker Street faced the school across the road.

Dr. ✓ No. 2 District. Part 1

John Street

The John Street entry in the 1867 Rate Book. 'H' means house, 'C' means cellar. The figures next to 'H' and 'C' are the approximate weekly rentals

In order to put flesh on the bones of these 'forgotten generations' it is necessary to search through a great many records.

The major source of information about the people of John Street are the census enumerators' returns for 1841 to 1891. These have obvious deficiencies and a deeper study reveals further inadequacies. The 1841 census is the most frustrating, since nearly half the pages which may be relevant to John Street are quite illegible. The enumerator visited the twenty-two dwellings at random and did not number them. Tenants shown by the rate books to have lived there are omitted, and names are included of people who lived elsewhere. Tenants who are known to have lived in adjacent houses are entered on the returns several pages apart. It is not possible to establish who lived in which house or how many people inhabited each one.

'An uncommon villain' and 'Jemmie the Crawler', two well known characters who were to be seen in and near Charter Street in 1867.

The 1851 census is a relief to use but completely omits 23 and 25 Parker Street. The 1861 census is difficult to read, but complete, as are those for 1871 and 1891; one house is omitted from the 1881 census.

The rate books are almost always extremely reliable, except in the early 1820s when development was so rapid that the assessors had great difficulty keeping up with it. New buildings were recorded without numbers, or under their landlords' names, or simply the comment 'building'. Only two years, 1855 and 1870, have major discrepancies and these are copying errors - every tenant is entered as living in the house next door to that which he really occupied. Somewhere, a clerk had omitted one number and displaced all the others by one.

Three kinds of confidence trickster to be seen in the Charter Street area. These 'Specimens of the countryman's obliging guides' are, left to right: 'The swell who has seen him before somewhere', 'The unemployed gent who will show him the town' and 'The straightforward John Bull who likes his face and is a farmer himself'.

The chief problem facing the researcher is that of accurate identification of houses when none of the maps ever gave a number to an individual property. Identification is made more difficult by the vagueness of the address given. Back Ashley Lane, for example, may be confused with the houses across the yard at the back of Ashley Lane, and may be listed as Back Ashley Lane, Back of Ashley Lane, Parker's Court (although there was a Parker's Court further up Parker Street) and sometimes simply as a court between two numbers on Parker Street. Since the numbers on Parker Street were changed three times during the first twenty-five years, this adds to the difficulty of finding Back Ashley Lane at all. Accurate identification of numbers is possible only by studying every one of the rate books. The plans on page 11 show the properties as they were between 1824 and 1911. The numbering system used for convenience throughout this account is that for 1853.

The average recorded tenancy in John Street was two years. The true figure was probably considerably less. Moving was easy when the total contents of one home could fit on a single handcart. People moved frequently but not very far. When rent arrears became too high, evictions or a moonlight flit would follow.

It is possible to establish tenancy patterns on an annual basis but there is some evidence that tenancies were frequently shorter than this. Some census returns give one name while the rate book may record two other names for the same house in one year. Since some cottages had the same tenant for a dozen or more years the 'average tenancy' of two years, based only on the names recorded in the rate books, is deceptive. Most tenancies were considerably shorter. Since the turnover amongst cellar tenants is seen from the rate books to have been higher than that of the cottage tenants, it can be assumed that the 'moonlight flit' was not unknown in John Street.

Cholera in Irk Town

These case histories of nine victims of cholera in Back Irk Street are taken from Dr Gaulter's report on the 'Origin and Progress of the Malignant Cholera in Manchester'. The north-easterly portion of his map is reproduced here.

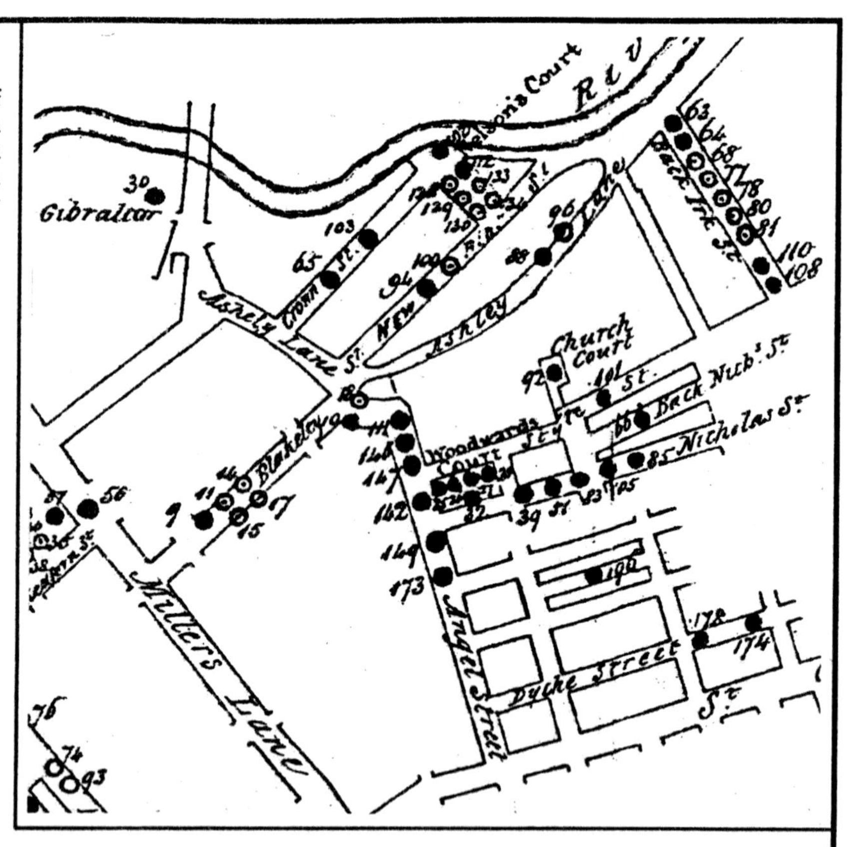

Dr Gaulter used the following abbreviations:
E - Employment
C - Constitution
N.S. Natural Susceptibility
P.C. Predisposing Cause
E.C. Exciting Cause
L.C.F. Locality, Crowding, Filth, &c
D.A. and E. Date of Attack and Event
P.S. Preliminary Symptoms
C. or N. Communication or Non-communication

Case No.63
Elizabeth Sharples, aged 63
52 Back Irk Street
E. stay-maker, but long out of employment. C. robust for her age. N.S. subject to a bowel complaint. P.C. half famished, lived on tea and bread, sober. E.C. none known, no error of diet. L.C.F. Street unlevelled; unpaved, the contents of the common sewer running above ground close past the door, the Irk a stone's throw from it, furnitureless house, four adults and three children lived in it half-starved and half-naked, sleeping all on the floor. D.A. and E. seized with P.S. Wednesday the 4th, collapse on Friday the 6th, died Saturday afternoon. C.N. said not to have been out of the house for three months, nobody ill in the vicinity, positively declares that there had been no communication direct or indirect with anybody ill.

Case No.64
Hugh Sharples, aged 4
52 Back Irk Street
Grandson of No.63. P.C. half starved, in rags. E.C. none known, no error of diet. L.C.F.&c. street unpaved the contents of the common sewer running above ground close past the door, the Irk a stone's throw from it, furnitureless house, four adults and three children lived in it half starved and half naked, sleeping all on the floor. D.A.E. seized at the same time as his grandmother on Wednesday the 4th. Died after hydrocephalic symptoms July 15th. C. or N. no communication whatever with any case out of the house and seized simultaneously with the grandmother.

Case No.67
Elizabeth Sharples, aged 34
Back Irk Street
E. a throstle spinner, grand-daughter of No.63. C. strong. P.C. (see case No.61) E.C. none known, no error of diet. L.C.F.&c. (see case No.63) D.A. and E. seized Friday the 6th at 8 a.m. died 8th on the Sunday night. C. or N. slept with No.63, while she was suffering from mild premonitory symptoms.

Case No.77
Thomas Sharples, aged 4
Back Irk Street
E. cousin to Hugh (case 64). L.C.F.&c. (see case 64). D.A.E. seized on Sunday 8th July, case mild one: not reported. C. or N. free communication with the others.

Case No.78
Elizabeth Draper, aged 3
Back Irk Street
E. cousin to Hugh (case 64). D.A.E. seized on Sunday morning 8th July, and recovered after severe hydrocephalic symptoms. C. or N. free communication with the others.

Case No.80
Sarah Dennis, aged 25
51, Back Irk Street
E. worked in a factory. C. short, moderately stout. N.S. not subject to diarrhoea. P.C. none known; sober; very poor. E.C. no error of diet. L.C.F.&c., see case 63. D.A.E. seized July 7th, recovered in four days. C. or N. see case 81.

Case No.81
Edward Dennis, aged 28
51, Back Irk Street, next door to case 63.
E. spinner. C. tall spare. N.S. none. P.C. very indigent. E.C. no error of diet. L.C.F.&c., for the locality see case 63. D.A.E. seized with P.S. Monday, July 9th, recovered after collapse, July 17. C. or N. his sister (case 80) had been into Sharples' during her illness; he had not, but stood at the door when the old woman was taken to the hospital.

Case No.108
Anne Hannah, aged 8
23 Back Irk Street
E. father a weaver. C. very fine girl. N.S. not subject to disordered bowels. P.C. (see case No.110.) E.C. had supped on porridge and buttermilk. L.C.F.&c. house furnitureless, dirty, containing six children and two adults, just opposite the house the common sewer discharges its contents which runs down the street for several hundred yards into the river, gas and ammonia works a little higher up. D.A.&E. seized Friday, July 20th, 7a.m. Died 10p.m. C. or N. had had positively no communication with the Dennis's or Sharples's in the same street.

Case No.110
Margaret Hannah, aged 3
23 Back Irk Street
E father a weaver. C. very fine girl. N.S. not subject to bowel complaints P.C. half famished, both the parents out of work for many weeks, in perfect health previously. E.C. none known. L.C.F.&c (see case No. 108.) D.A.&E. seized Monday, July 23rd, 7a.m. died the same day at 5. C. or N. her sister had been removed to the hospital so soon that Margaret did not see her after her illness being out at play: did not see her after death, nor come in contact with the bed or clothes she had used.

Life in Irk Town

The Early Decades

Even before the back-to-back houses were built, when only 4 to 8 John Street and 46 and 48 Back Irk Street, with their cellars and back houses, existed, the area was already a slum. Dr Gaulter, anxious, as were so many other doctors in 1832, to discover the cause of cholera, described the circumstances of the nine cholera victims a few yards away in Back Irk Street. At 23 lived the Hannah family, the adults unemployed weavers, the six children *'half famished'*. They had no furniture and outside their house the open sewer discharged its infected contents, which passed the doors and cellar areas of 46 and 48 Back Irk Street on their way to the river. The effect can clearly be seen on Gaulter's cholera map. The Sharples family of four adults and three children lived at 52, *'half-starved and half-naked, sleeping all on the floor.'* Elizabeth Sharples, an unemployed stay-maker, and two of her grandchildren died.

Since Irk Town lay midway between Angel Meadow and Irish Town, it is not surprising that many of John Street's tenants were Irish, often described as 'weavers' rather than 'weaver by power' or 'powerloom weaver', as were many others in the 1841 census returns for this enumeration district. Some Irish families were recent immigrants, with some children born in Ireland and the very young ones born in England. Twenty-two people seem to have lived in 46 and 48 Back Irk Street; occupations are entered for fourteen. Of these, eleven were weavers ranging in age from 65 to 12, and of both sexes.

The two remaining larger houses, without cellars, were rented to Englishmen, one a constable and one a smith, both the sole wage earners, although the constable had a twelve-year-old son who could have been contributing to the family income. None of the tenants of the small back-to-backs from the John Street side can be found, except Arthur Higgins with his wife and two children. He was a plumber and the 1841 directory shows that he had another address at Flag Row. Indeed, their third child, Martha, was born at Flag Row in August. Only one Back Ashley Lane tenant is included, Ralph Brown, a shoemaker with a wife and baby and two aged parents of 80 and 70. Mr Brown senior is one of only two octogenarians recorded in any census for John Street, although a letter in the 'Manchester Courier' of January 7th 1843 describes a New Year's party given at St Michael's School for one hundred of the oldest inhabitants of the area. One of the party-goers was Martha Wood aged 92 of John Street, not recorded in the census return, although Woods lived at 6 and 8 John Street in 1841. The 'churchman' who wrote the letter considered that their longevity depended upon their characters and the fear of the Lord, even in the *'polluted air of a manufacturing town'*. Since most of the guests must have been born before 1770, it is likely that 'pure country air', a factor which he considered unimportant, had more to contribute to their longevity than piety; most of them must have been immigrants, since Manchester's population in 1770 was only about 25,000.

It is extremely rare to find a source which mentions an inhabitant of John Street by name, and none has the human interest of the aged persons' party which Martha Wood attended. There are but three entries in St Michael's parish registers and a handful in St Patrick's, the main Roman Catholic church for the thousands of Irish in Ancoats, Newtown, Irk Town, Irish

Itinerant coal dealers, a familiar sight in and around Charter Street during the mid-nineteenth century.

Town and Angel Meadow. So few of the tenants of John Street appear in these registers that it seems likely that the English, in particular, were baptised, married and buried outside the established Church.

The burial register of St Michael's records the burial on May 10th 1842 of Mary Foulkes, the wife of the smith at 1 John Street. It may be that her death was related to childbearing, as the census of 1841 showed her to have had four children of nine, six, four and seven months. Thomas moved to the smaller house next door after her death and went away the following year. He was not recorded in a Manchester directory after that.

There are two baptismal records of children born to John Street people: on November 6th 1850 Margaret, daughter of Thomas Flavel, a dyer and his wife Ann, of 2 Back Ashley Lane; then a long gap until the baptism on April 7th 1872 of Mary Ann, daughter of William Newbury, a mechanic, and his wife Harriet of 23 Parker Street.

St Patrick's registers are more fruitful, recording one baptism, of Michael Barns, son of John and Mary of 10 Back Ashley Lane, on March 24th 1839, and several burials and marriages. There are identification problems in the burial registers as there were two John Streets between the river and Rochdale Road; where 'John Street' is followed by 'Newtown' or 'Irk Town' then there is no problem, but other John Street entries may refer to either. The mortality in John Street and Silver Court, at the back of the Griffin houses, was high, with five deaths being recorded between 1845 and July 1846, and January 1853 to 1858. Four of the deaths were of children between five weeks and two years, and one was that of a 52-year-old woman, of a 'decline'. Other entries are for an unspecified John Street, and the causes of deaths for John Street and Silver Court include measles, chin cough, teeth, old age, inflammation, asthma, convulsions and cough. Leigh and Gardiner's cholera map of 1849 shows that the area was as badly affected as it had been in 1832, but the burial registers for 1849 are missing.

'The dealer in bitters', another Charter Street character.

Ashley Lane Sunday School in 1972. The ground floor was built in 1827 as a mission of the Grosvenor Street Chapel near Piccadilly. The building was extended in 1844. It became a day school, first for infants and then a Board school in 1872.

How important Back Ashley Lane Day and Sunday Schools were to John Street cannot be known. Although many of the children in the 1851, 1861, 1871 1881 and 1891 census returns are described as 'scholars', there is no way of knowing which school they attended or whether this was a conventional term to describe a child of school age. The Sunday School Registers have not survived and the Sunday School Teachers' Minute Book never mentions a pupil by name.

The Minute Book does, however, preserve the particulars of the entry for the census return of March 30th 1851. The attendance for that afternoon was 406, of whom 204 were also Day School scholars, and 190 former Day School scholars. Writing, being considered work, was not taught at the Sunday School - it was Independent - but grammar and geography were taught on a week night, and the Minute Book makes it clear that there was a mid-week writing class. The return of the Manchester Sunday School Union in 1853 is more illuminating. The teachers themselves followed up and visited their own absentees; 60 scholars borrowed books from the library; there were evening classes, a sick relief fund, a clothing fund, a juvenile Mission fund and a Young Men's Mutual Improvement class.

Until 1840 the annual Whitsuntide outing was to Dunham, but in that year the Directors of the Manchester and Leeds Railway Company offered to take scholars to Mill Hill for 3d each. The trip must have been successful as it was repeated annually. On the Friday of Whit Week there was always a local outing and picnic, sometimes to Collyhurst Clough, or to Newton Grange, Smedley or even the Cheetham Hill garden of one of the richer members of the congregation. The scholars paid 4d for their picnic in 1842 and had the pleasure of six balloons. It was usual to get the boys to the venue an hour before the girls, presumably to allow them to work off a little energy first. There was always a New Year tea party for parents and teachers, at 4d for parents and 6d for teachers. The people of John Street must have had some lighter moments between unemployment, sickness and burials. Whitsun 1847 brought a change, with an offer of hospitality from the Chapel at Tintwistle in Derbyshire, which was accepted, and returned later in the year. It would be interesting to know what the children of Tintwistle made of Irk Town, with its railway, mills, gas works and evil-smelling river. John Street could not have been a pleasant place in which to live, even when the houses were new.

Life in Irk Town

The Middle Decades

The census return of 1851 for the twenty-three dwellings shows that some changes had taken place in the last decade, particularly in employment patterns. Many more people worked in factories, although there were still two handloom weavers and many cap makers. William Hall of 6 John Street, a weaver in 1848, was a baker and shopkeeper; his was the commercial premises marked on Adshead's map (below). The household at 5 John Street was particularly curious: George and Nancy Coulson and their one-year-old daughter Harriet were all born in Warsaw, Poland; their four-month-old baby was born in Manchester. George was a glazier and employed a fifteen-year-old Irish girl as a servant. The question of where, in a one-up, one-down cottage Mary Flannigan would sleep, presents itself. George left John Street the next year and cannot be traced in subsequent directories.

A doll maker from Stockport, Charles Cumberbirch, his wife, baby and brother, a porter, lived at 1 John Street. Across the road, next to William Hall's shop, was a house with a cellar dwelling which contained the Riley family and eleven lodgers,

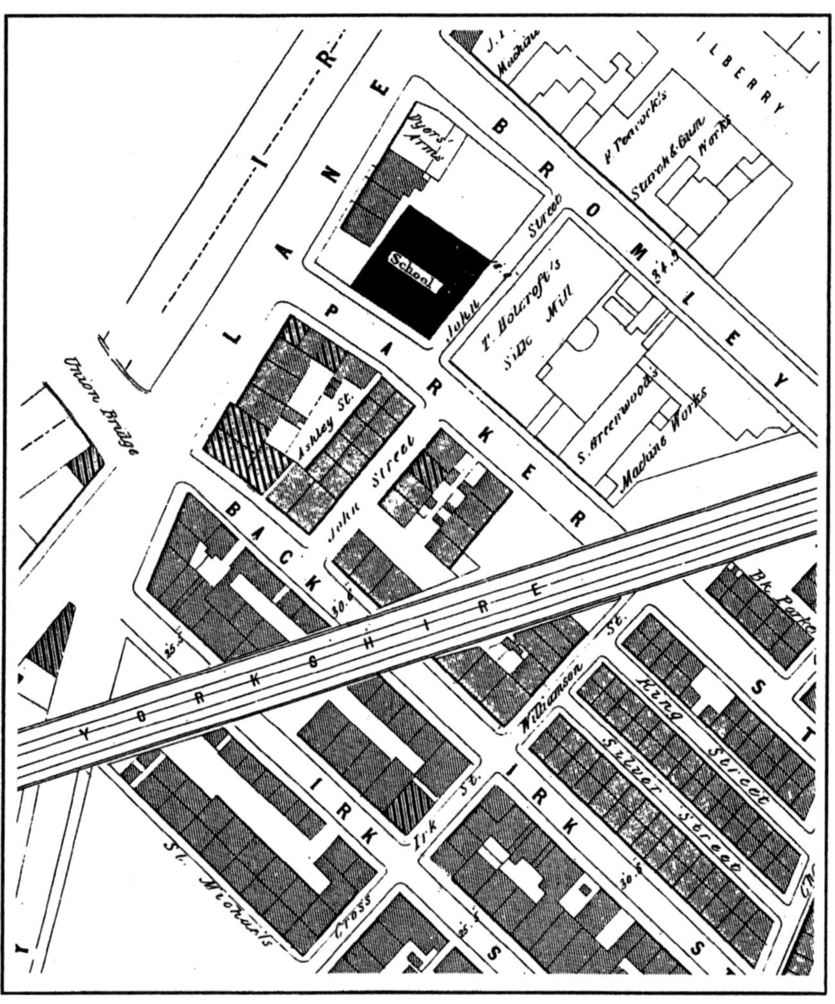

Adshead's map of 1851. Commercial premises are striped. No.6 John Street was a bakery and shop at that time. Siddy's establishment on Ashley Lane was substantial.

all Irish. In all, nineteen people inhabited 4 John Street. Of twenty-six heads of families, fourteen were Irish. The housing density was very high: 7.07 for the district, 7.44 per house for John Street.

During the 1850s the sanitary movement was gaining in strength and in 1853 and 1854 members of the Rochdale Road Committee of the Manchester and Salford Sanitary Association visited the area. They made three comments on John Street's inhabitants; they had insufficient *'petty accommodation'*, their houses were *'completely overcrowded'* and their habits were *'in most cases very offensive'*. Their observations concerning overcrowding in John Street and Back Ashley Lane are borne out by the figures given above.

In spite of this unfavourable report, the people of John Street were in some ways better off than others in the neighbourhood. None of them shared their cellar dwelling with a donkey, as someone in Nicholas Street did, and insufficient 'petty accommodation' was better than none at all. Four houses at 25 Flag Row were in this predicament. *'It is as well,'* commented the Inspectors, *'that a railroad is at hand where the people say they have Recourse in their Extremity.'* In spite of the Manchester Police Act of 1844, which had made the building of back-to-backs an offence, the committee noted that Pilling's Buildings in Newtown consisted of twelve new houses, being built back-to-back. The owner was an alderman on the new City Council.

Looking across St Michael's Flags, the former Parish Burial Ground, from under the railway on Ashley Lane in 1899. Back-to-backs in Style Street can be seen beyond St Michael's Church.

The inspectors also noted, with some indignation, the condition of the Parish Burial Ground, closed and neglected for many years and by 1854 in a *'sad and disgraceful condition'*. The only open space for a considerable distance, it afforded a *'scene of constant gambling and fighting, particularly on the Lord's Day.'* The space was also a particularly useful place for the disposal of refuse of every kind.

The Sanitary Association not only inspected for nuisances but also involved itself in education, running a series of public lectures in the mid-1850s on such topics as 'Respiration and Food' and 'The Physical and Moral Evils arising from Weather, Heat, Cold, Damp, want of Light, Cellar and Court Residences &c' at St Michael's School. The working class was warmly invited to these lectures, as were the mothers of families.

Other improvements being introduced into the area included the Ragged Schools - Sharp Street and Angel Meadow, later called Charter Street.

The 1850s also provide the only evidence concerning the marriages of John Street people. St Patrick's Marriage Registers record five marriages between 1858 and 1860, which seem to show that Irk Town people did not look very far for their marriage partners. On June 1st 1858 Patrick Courtney of John Street married Bridget Canterran of Gould Street. Their witnesses included Patrick Walsh of Silver Court. On October 24th Patrick Barrett of Silver Court married Catherine McCormick of John Street and the following year John Fitzpatrick of No.2 took a wife from Back Irk Street. 1860 saw the marriages of Patrick Hughes and Mary Lappin, both of John Street, and Patrick Garry from No.4 with Catherine Burke of Silver Street. Patrick and Catherine's witnesses were both from Silver Court.

The 1861 census returns show that, at least at the time of the census, overcrowding was considerably reduced both in the district, where it was 5.69, and in John Street, where it was 5.94 per house. Pressure on housing accommodation must have been great though, since there were only three uninhabited houses in the district, one more than in 1851.

most detrimental to the health, as well as the morals, of the people."

Back Ashley Lane
Silver St. Court
John St.
Back of John St
King St.
Charlotte St
Back Parker St

} All these streets have not sufficient Petty accommodations. Many of the houses completely overcrowded, & the habits of the people in most cases very offensive.

Part of the 1854 report of the Rochdale Road Committee of the Manchester and Salford Sanitary Association.

Employment patterns had changed again during the decade. By 1861 only two people were engaged in domestic trades, both mothers of young children, one as a shirt maker and the other a cap maker. The only person with semi-professional status was William Lewis, an overlooker in a silk mill, and since the rate book for 1861 has the comment that Tryall Holcroft of Holcroft's silk mill, once Parker's mill, was bankrupt, and had no effects with which to pay the rates, it seems very likely that William Lewis could have become unemployed that year. Lewis's house, in any case, contained two lodgers, one an unmarried woman of 43, born on St Helena.

The street still housed a large number of Irish people and though now only 12 heads of the 27 households were Irish, many of the lodgers still were. The Welsh family is one example. Bridget Welsh, a fifty-year-old widow from Galway, lived in one of the back-to-backs with three unmarried sons between 21 and 16, and in the cellar of No.8 lived Michael Welsh and his wife Margaret, both 30, with one eight-year old son, though three of the John Street children whose burials were recorded at St Patrick's in 1854 were called Welsh. Upstairs lived James Byrns, a musician, from Ireland, with his wife and seven-year-old son and baby daughter. With only seven people in one of the Griffin houses and cellar it must have seemed quite spacious.

Apart from Holcroft's bankruptcy, which must have affected the employment of more than William Lewis since nine other people were recorded in the census as being silk workers, the main recorded event of the 1860s in the area was the long public hearing over the scandalous condition of the Parish Burial Ground. This followed a letter written by Dr Meacham, the Medical Officer of St George's District, to Lord Shaftesbury on November 1st 1866. In it he mentioned that *'occasionally a human skull is turned up and thrown about; more than forty thousand dead lay there, yet not a gravestone is left; some may be found forming part of the floor of cottages, others may be seen placed in privies.'*

In his evidence Mr Cliffe, the churchwarden, said that the wall had begun to give way as early as 1830 and that it gave way completely opposite St Michael's Place. It may in that

Two 'one-armed travellers' who had an up-and-down fight on the Parish Burial Ground. This dirty fight attracted a large crowd.

case have deposited its contents in the yard of Eleazar Siddy's first bakery. The burial ground had since then been used for the burning of fever beds, the depositing of mussels, for cat and dog fights and the tipping of refuse from the gas works. 'Greengorse' said early in the decade that he had seen an 'up-and-down' fight between *'two one-armed "travellers", which took place upon this ground. "Bacup Billy", a "kerbstone collier", was a merry rogue who had many admirers. "Stumpy", a lodging-house "depitty", once a "navvy", was his opponent.'*

It had long been the desire of the Rev J R Mercer, the incumbent of St Michael's, to convert this open space into a children's playground. Central Manchester was most deficient in this respect. Queen's Park in Harpurhey, although opened in 1846, was a long walk from Irk Town. The playgrounds which the Corporation provided in Ancoats and other districts were not opened until the clearance of small slum areas following the 1890 Housing of the Working Classes Act. No wonder, then, that the turbulent population of Irk Town, Newtown and Angel Meadow adopted the disused burial ground for their rough recreational pursuits. It was finally closed and renamed St Michael's Flags in 1868.

The investigations of sanitary reformers had had no effect on John Street by the late 1860s. The 1871 census shows it as bad as it had ever been. Overcrowding was very serious and the social status of the inhabitants lower than ever. The enumeration district now included Dimity Street and Flag Row, notorious slums, and this may have adversely affected the figures on average conditions in the district compared with those of previous decades. There were 176 inhabited houses, seven unoccupied, with a housing density of 4.98. In John Street it was 6.67. No.2 Back Ashley Lane, although only a one up, one down, housed two families. Similarly, one of the John Street back-to-backs housed James Fallon, a gas worker, his wife and three very young children, and another household of Irish people, a fifty-year-old widower, his thirteen-year-old son and an unrelated man of sixty. The other back-to-backs contained one family each.

It was worse in the larger

Charter Street Ragged School seen through the abandoned swings of St Michael's Flags in 1917. Perhaps the war was responsible.

Griffin houses. At No.4 was John McCormick, aged 50 and blind; he described himself as a calico printer and had lived in John Street since at least 1858, when his daughter Catherine married Patrick Barrett from around the corner in Silver Court. In 1861 he was living in the cellar of No.4 and was described as 'formerly a mat maker' and 'blind 4 years'. He had three daughters at home then and had acquired another by 1871. Two of them were flax spinners. The cellar housed four lodgers, all widowed people, of both sexes, aged between 43 and 70, and not related to each other.

St Michael's Flags in the 1960s, abandoned for the second time in its history.

Next door also had an occupied cellar and a family and boarders in the house, and the conditions in No.8 must have been quite dreadful. Michael Norton, a 35-year-old Irish cabinet maker with a wife, a son of twelve (a blacking maker), a ten-year-old daughter (a nurse, probably a child minder), sons of six and three, daughters of four and one, a mother-in-law of 54, a 56-year-old boarder and her 21-year-old son all lived in the house. In the cellar was the Flaherty family with five children ranging from fifteen to two months; No.8 John Street gave shelter to 19 people.

The listed occupations of John Street's people are a monotonous recital of labourers, cabinet makers, a mangle-turner and more labourers. There was no-one involved in any form of retail trade nor in a skilled or semi-skilled occupation. Sixteen out of twenty-five heads of households were Irish. John Street had slipped even further down the social scale than it had been before.

St Michael's Flags newly landscaped in 1982. This was the second time that the New Burial Ground had been rehabilitated.

Life in Irk Town

The Closing Decades

Steady pressure from sanitary reformers, both local and national, led to John Leigh's appointment as Medical Officer of Health. His three-pronged attack on Manchester's appalling mortality rates included the removal of midden privies, the closure of cellar dwellings and the reconditioning of substandard cottage property. There is no direct evidence of the conversion of midden to pail privies in John Street, although the 1889 25-inch Ordnance Survey map shows rather more than had been apparent in 1850.

T R Marr, reporting for the Citizens' Association for the Improvement of the Unwholesome Dwellings and Surroundings of the People found, in 1904, that all the closets inspected were pail closets except for a small number of W.Cs. As the construction of pail closets had officially been discouraged since 1890, it may be assumed that John Street obtained this more sanitary form of closet before they were finally condemned.

Census returns and the rate book show that cellar dwellings were still occupied, and overcrowded, in 1871. Leigh had closed down all but a hundred or so by 1872 and John Street's cellars were no longer occupied in 1873 - John Street must have been amongst the last to receive the attention of the Medical Officer. The landlord lost 1/3d each per week in rent for the Griffin houses but neither he nor Manchester's rating department was compensated, since rental and rateable values of the houses did not increase in the next years.

It has already been seen that the cellars were very overcrowded and their closure raises the question of where the displaced cellar dwellers went. In one case the answer is known, because Patrick Flaherty took his family across the road to Back Ashley Lane, with an estimated rental of 2/6d a week. Since he had three employed teenage children in 1871 it may be that he lived in a cellar not because he wished to, but because he could find no where else until 4 Back Ashley Lane became vacant. Alternatively, he may have found the rent too much, because he had gone away from his new home by 1874.

Ashley Lane British School was transferred to the School Board in September 1872, perhaps indicating a financial struggle to keep it going. On the other hand, the Sunday School proudly celebrated its golden

T R Marr illustrated his 1904 book 'Housing Conditions in Manchester and Salford' with several photographs taken in St Michael's Ward. These houses are similar to 4, 6 and 8 John Street, built with cellar dwellings. Later improvements would have provided the closets seen here, and the tap on which the little girl is resting her hand.

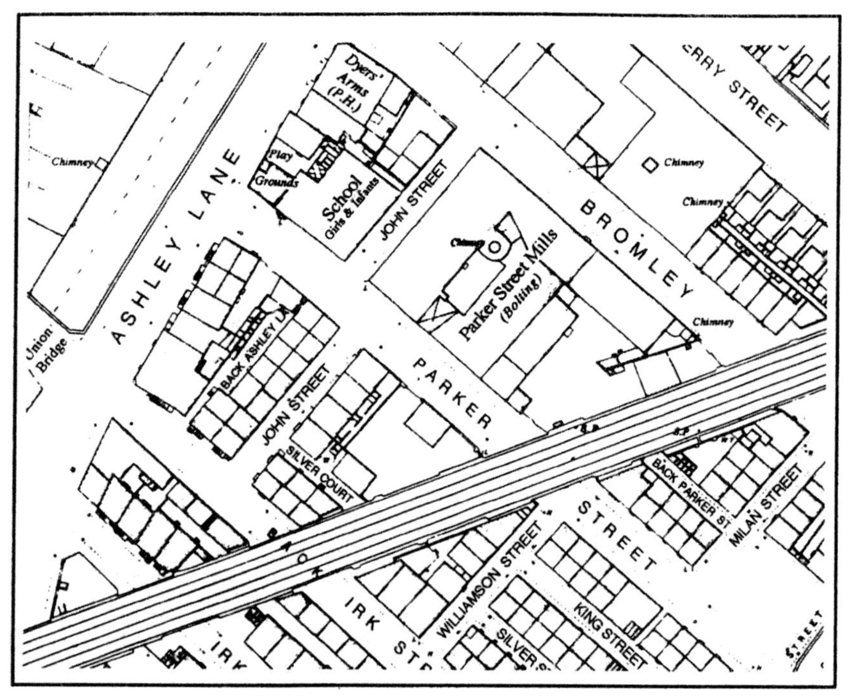

The 1889 Ordnance Survey map. The only improvement in forty years was an increase in the number of privies.

jubilee in October 1875, with a splendid tea party and speeches reflecting pride in fifty years' growth and service.

The 1881 census shows little difference from earlier decades. The occupations of its inhabitants were quite as lowly, though more varied in range, as they had been ten years earlier. There were considerably fewer textile workers but three women farriers, a skinner, three preserve makers, a coachman and a hair opener were amongst those employed. Domestic trades were represented by an umbrella maker (a mother of young children), a cabinet maker and a cap maker. There were several labourers. Julia Burke at 7 John Street had an occupation which must, considering the area, have been particularly unpleasant; she was a rag sorter. The number of uninhabited houses was six out of 177, with an average housing density of 5.18. At last, for the first time in thirty years or more, John Street, with exactly five per house, was less overcrowded than the average for the district. The closure of the cellar dwellings accounts for the change. There were still eleven Irish out of the seventeen heads of household

Brushmaking was typical of the putting-out trades of the nineteenth century. Women and children worked long hours, often for starvation wages. Brushmakers lived in John Street in 1851 and 1861.

Census Returns 1851-1891

Since the numbers of people involved in the study are very small, broad employment categories have been used, following the pattern used by John Smith in 'Ten Acres of Deansgate in 1861', published in the 'Transactions of the Lancashire and Cheshire Antiquarian Society', 1980. To his list of categories one other has been added, namely 'labourer'. Where the particular industry of a labourer is known, i.e., 'farm labourer', he has been included under 'agriculture'.

Construction	includes carpenter, glazier, plumber, bricklayer, brickmaker, painter
Clothing	includes all needle trades, seamstress, tailor, capmaker, umbrella maker
Domestic	includes servant, nurse, laundress, mangle, char
Power	includes gas, coal
Furnishing	includes cabinet maker
Leather	includes shoe maker, boot maker
Metal	includes foundry worker, farrier
Miscellaneous	musician, hair opener, hawker, rag sorter, clay pipe maker, brush maker, button turner
Paper	includes paper making, printing
Retail	shopkeeper, baker, beer retailer, preserve maker
Semi-professional	overlooker
Textile	carding, scavenging, spinning, weaving, winding, dyeing, printing
Transport, warehousing	porter, warehouseman, packer, maker-up
Children	aged 5 or over, not described as scholars
Small Children	aged below 5

(Since the census enumerators' returns omit some houses the number of John Street houses assessed is not the same for each year and is as follows:- 1851-16, 1861-18, 1871-18, 1881-17, 1891-10)

	1851	1861	1871	1881	1891
Agriculture	-	-	5	-	-
Construction	6	2	7	1	4
Clothing	10	3	6	2	3
Domestic	1	1	4	3	4
Power	-	-	2	1	-
Furnishing	2	-	2	2	-
General Labourers	4	6	11	15	3
Leather	2	-	-	-	2
Metal	-	4	4	4	-
Miscellaneous	3	5	6	9	2
Paper	1	-	2	-	-
Retail	2	2	-	3	1
Semi-professional	-	1	-	-	-
Textile	26	31	12	7	2
Transport, Warehouse	2	7	5	4	1
Women at home not working	14	12	17	8	6
Wives working	6	8	5	4	5
People over 12 not working (excluding wives)	7	3	1	1	2
Paupers, pensioners	2	-	-	-	-
Scholars	12	13	22	9	4
Children 5 - 10	4	3	4	7	5
Small children 0 - 4	19	13	14	9	10
Single income families	3	7	7	2	2

Comparison of housing totals between enumeration district (Dist) and John Street (John):

	1851		1861		1871		1881		1891	
	Dist	John	Dist	John	Dist	John	Dist	John	Dist	John
No. of schedules	151	21	168	31	191	25	194	17	191	9
No. of inhabited houses	133	16	121	18	176	18	177	17	193	9
No. of uninhabited houses	2	0	3	0	7	0	6	0	19	4
No. of males	441	57	319	51	409	62	427	34	429	22
No. of females	499	62	396	56	467	58	488	51	457	25
No. of total	940	119	688	107	876	120	917	85	886	47
Average no. of people per schedule	6.23	5.67	4.09	3.45	4.49	4.8	4.72	5	4.6	5.2
Average no. of people per house	7.07	7.44	5.69	5.94	4.98	6.67	5.18	5	4.6	5.2

Origin and sex of heads of household:

This total includes boarders or lodgers who form a complete family within the same schedule in 1851.

*Within 3 to 4 miles of present centre of Manchester

	1851	1861	1871	1881	1891
Local*	9	10	6	4	7
Irish	14	12	16	2	0
Other	3	5	3	11	4
Male	17	22	23	11	9
Female	9	5	2	6	2
Total	26	27	25	17	11

(one house was omitted by the census enumerator in 1881).

Leigh's battle against disease and high mortality was not showing the desired reduction and pressure was being brought to bear on the Sanitary Committee and the Medical Officer of Health to introduce water-borne sanitation. Leigh was aware of the enormous cost of introducing such a system and of the problem of river pollution, which was rendered greater every time a water closet added its contents to the sewers. In his report of 1883 he mentioned that the sewers below Bilberry and Parker Streets discharged their contents into the Irk.

The Unhealthy Dwellings Sub-Committee of the Sanitary Committee inspected a great many dwellings in Manchester between 1885 and 1890 and recommended action in most of the cases upon which it reported. Reconditioning of some back-to-back houses took place and the conversion to through houses of the middle, but not the end cottages, was completed by 1891. The Griffin houses were unoccupied by 1888. Two of them were already empty in 1887, but there is no indication of the reason. Various possibilities suggest themselves; that the Lancashire and Yorkshire Railway Company had bought them prior to the widening of the viaduct, or that the Unhealthy Dwellings Committee had ordered their closure and Thomas Vickers was not prepared to spend money on houses built sixty years earlier.

Reconditioning of all but 46 Back Irk Street, 1 John Street and 23 and 25 Parker Street was completed by 1891. 1 John Street remained the only true back-to-back until it was condemned with the others in 1903. The other three all had two outside walls which would enable additional windows to be inserted, to permit through ventilation, although there is no evidence that they were.

1891 is the latest year for which census returns are available. At the time of the enumeration the houses were in the process of reconditioning; indeed, 9 John Street and 10 Back Ashley Lane were actually unoccupied at the time, though tenanted as two dwellings in 1890 and one in 1892. The three Griffin houses were boarded up, although No.2, built later in 1839, was still occupied. Some of the back-to-backs had been converted to through houses, including Henry Evans' four, and Miss Siddy's 48 Back Irk Street, built in 1824, now combined with its original back house.

The other corner houses were still one-up-one-downs, and 1 John Street was still a true back-to-back, incapable of through ventilation. Henry Evans now had new tenants, the eight Wrights at No.3 and Margaret O'Donnell, the widowed charwoman, her five-year-old daughter and her lodgers, John and Margaret Heaton at No.5. Miss Siddy's No.7 housed the five Waldens and their lodgers, a family of three. No.2 across the road was occupied by the fish hawkers, George and

Coke, a byproduct of the gasworks, being sold to local people in 1894. Children of the poorest families picked up the hot bits that fell from the carts as they left the works.

Elizabeth Oakley. Ann Dunn, the 54-year-old widowed charwoman who had lived at No.6 in 1881 was still renting it, although when it was closed she had gone to live round the back in Silver Court. In 1893 she crossed the road and moved into Miss Siddy's surviving back-to-back at 1 John Street, remaining there till it was condemned ten years later.

By 1891 the twenty-one dwellings occupied in 1844 were down to eleven. The two cellars had been closed in 1872 and the three Griffin houses by 1888. Five back-to-backs had disappeared in creating five new two-up, two-downs. Four one-up, one downs and the two late infills remained. The average density had increased to 5.2 against the district's 4.6, showing that the improvement in 1881 had been a temporary respite. Two of the one-up-one-downs had only two occupants each. The others had five, six and seven inhabitants respectively. Of the four-roomed houses, two had eight inhabitants, one had four, and the other, five.

A Ragged School teacher commented in 1892 on the benefits children derived from the conversion of the pauper burial ground to a playground. It was still serving the same useful purpose in 1914, as this photograph taken on St Michael's Flags shows.

In 1891 two circumstances show significant differences from previous censuses. The first concerns the places of birth of the tenants. Of the forty-seven in 1891, not one was born in Ireland, though names such as Bridget and O'Donnell indicate families of Irish origin. Thirty-six of the tenants were born in Manchester, the remaining eleven in other parts of England. The second concerns the children. Of the twenty aged thirteen and under, seven were aged four and below, and were at home; of the remaining thirteen, only three were described as scholars, representing fifteen per cent, by far the lowest percentage of any of the other census years.

Employment patterns were little changed from previous years, with no skilled workers, with the possible exception of a shoe maker. Only two people were engaged in the textile industry. Needle trades were represented by a tailoress, married to a button turner, and most unusually, by two men, one a furrier of sixteen and the other a thirty-year-old cap maker, living with his widowed mother. The most unpleasant occupation was probably that of the sixteen-year-old tan yard assistant.

The tenants of John Street were left alone for another decade following the closure and reconditioning of 1887-1891, but closure and reconditioning continued all around. In his Statistical Society lecture of 1897, the Rev. Mercer mentioned that in the St Michael's district 381 dwellings had been demolished or reconditioned and 120 reconditioned and provided with yards and W.Cs in the previous year. This activity and the extensions of the railway and warehouses had caused the population to decline, although the housing density in the remaining dwellings did not, of course, decline with it.

The area had not changed its character during the course of the century. A feature by 'Rambler' in the 'Manchester City News' in 1892 remarked on the vacancies in the Working Girls' Home attached to Charter Street Ragged School, although the rents of 1/3d per week included baths, communal living room, kitchen, laundry and private rooms - unheard of luxury in that area. He considered that the restrictions imposed upon the girls may have been unpopular enough to explain the vacancies: *'it takes a long time to tame an Angel Meadow girl,'* he said. It is unlikely that John Street girls were very different.

The same paper in the following week published a letter from a Ragged School teacher, noting with approval the benefits the children had derived from the conversion of the burial ground to St Michael's Flags, but the Rev. Mercer was still very much aware of how much remained for him to do. He hoped to open St Michael's Church Yard for the use of adults. He knew there was nowhere else for the men to smoke their pipes and the women to do their knitting: *'At present they are compelled to cluster at street corners or sit on the doorsteps of the dusty, hot, narrow streets, often close to yawning sewers.'*

A yawning sewer had killed five people in Back Irk Street in 1832. The mortality rate in No.6 Sanitary District (John Street was practically on the boundary between No.6 and No.7) was still 50.9. compared with a national figure of below 19.

The final word picture of the area during the years of John Street's residential period comes from Arthur G Symonds in an article in the 'East Lancashire Review' of 1899. He had considered the eventful history of the Flags, which even in 1899 still had its colourful moments, particularly at election times. Standing with his back to them, looking up Irk Street, he saw *'one of those everyday sights so eloquent of the extreme poverty of this district, and of the struggle for life that is ceaselessly waged within its borders. Down the street came two carts from the gas works, piled up with coke, still warm and steaming. Behind each of them ran, or walked, or toddled, a dozen little children, all carrying bags, baskets, tin pails - anything that would serve as a receptacle - picking up the coke that fell from the carts as they jolted along.'*

One of the few streets in Ashley Field still inhabited in 1931. These were one up, one down dwellings and two of them housed families of seven, and one housed nine people.

Gaulter had described similar poverty in Back Irk Street in 1832. The relentless struggle against poverty and ill-health in John Street, however, was coming to an end. The last tenants' names are entered in the 1902 rate book but the 1903 book contains a terse note in red ink, 'condemned, 3rd Jan'. The last tenant moved into another of Miss Siddy's properties at the back of Ashley Lane. No-one else ever lived in John Street and the buildings were now known as 100 Gould Street or 25 Parker Street. The Deutsche Gemeinde Mission had moved in by 1904. It was after 1909 that a new floor was installed in the old 46 and 48 Back Irk Street, which filled in the cellars and provided a bed for the huge iron heating boiler removed by the last tenant when he took over the building.

The people who remained in Irk Town must have become increasingly lonely; the rate books for the next four years are full of closure notices. Industries which moved into the area were quite as unpleasant as the old ones. The Parlane Waterproof Company, occupying the site of 23 and 25 Parker Street, did not make the air smell any sweeter and members of the Manchester and Salford Better Housing Council who investigated the area in 1931 commented unfavourably on the smell.

It may be that John Street's last tenants were better off than those who remained to pay rent to landlords who, for the next thirty years, expected their property to be condemned and could see little point in keeping it in repair. One woman said sadly that the houses which remained were like 'withered trees'. The recommendation of the visiting committee was for total demolition and clearance.

John Street had never been a pleasant place in which to live. The Irk was less than fifty yards away, receiving the contents of the sewers under Bilberry and Parker Streets in 1883, Back Irk Street in 1832 and probably afterwards, and also the discharge from all the industries along the river, including the mills and the gas works. The mills, gas works, iron foundry on Red Bank, pig cotes and privies must have made Irk Town smell appalling. The poverty described by Gaulter in 1832 continued, to be noted by Symonds in 1899, and the census returns throughout the second half of the century refer to unemployment. The social status of the tenants had declined steadily in the same period. Swindells, in his 'Manchester Streets and Manchester Men', said, *'the change from open country to slums was carried out with almost startling rapidity in the Ashley Lane district.'*

John Street and Back Ashley Lane certainly confirm Swindells' observation. The deterioration was just as rapid. Built a slum, it remained a slum and no efforts of sanitary or philanthropic reformers could or did change it.

Charter Street in 1899 at the time of the construction of the Ragged School. Siddy's bakery is beyond the cart.

John Street and Nineteenth Century Housing Policy

The experience of John Street must have been repeated endlessly in slums all over Manchester. John Street may have been slightly better than some and worse than others, but the pattern echoes the story of working class housing in industrial Manchester as outlined by Manchester's two historians, Arthur Redford and Lady Shena Simon - John Street was a typical Manchester slum.

Throughout the nineteenth century the problems associated with the housing of the urban working classes were inextricably entwined in the minds of reformers with sanitary improvement. The association was natural, since doctors were the first influential group to become aware of the problems of slum dwellers during fever and cholera epidemics. It took the best part of the century to eradicate the epidemics and to improve insanitary living conditions and it then became dismayingly apparent that the housing problem remained.

In Manchester the formation of the Board of Health in 1796 and the establishment of a fever hospital familiarised doctors with the living conditions of the poor. It enabled them to predict accurately which parts of the town would be worst affected by cholera in 1832. Dr James Phillips Kay ensured that at least some leading citizens were involved in his investigations into the moral and sanitary condition of the working classes in Manchester, and these men became active in the sanitary movement of the town in the 1840s and 1850s.

Edwin Chadwick, a leading figure in the Sanitary Movement, who had hoped that a reduction of the poor rates would follow the implementation of the 1834 Poor Law Amendment Act, had reluctantly come to the conclusion that state intervention was necessary before any such reduction was possible. Illness and premature mortality were the main causes of pauperism; dirty living conditions caused the illness and death. Chadwick, once an exponent of laissez-faire, launched a crusade against dirt. He sent Kay and two other doctors to investigate some of the poorer parts of London. Their findings led him to make a detailed nationwide investigation which resulted in his report on the 'Sanitary Condition of the Labouring Population of Great Britain' in 1842. What Kay had found in Manchester in 1832, Chadwick's investigators found all over the country a decade later.

Whenever sanitary arrangements, water supply, drainage and houses were most unsatisfactory or inadequate, disease, chronic ill-health and premature and high mortality were greatest. Two years later a Royal Commission on the Health of Towns reported. Since Chadwick claimed to

The viaduct in 1894 crossing the slum which had been Ashley Field a century earlier. It passes within six yards of John Street.

have written two-thirds of the report himself, it is hardly surprising that its findings confirmed the 1842 report. The Health of Towns Association, comprising doctors and such distinguished philanthropists as Lord Ashley, was founded in 1844 and the sanitary movement became respectable. Although opposed by landowners, ratepayers, water companies and other vested interests, the movement gathered strength in the 1840s, fuelled by the irrefutable connection between the worst living conditions and the highest mortality.

The return of cholera in 1848 and 1849 gave the sanitary movement a further stimulus. Its strength was such that most reforming activity in the housing field until the 1880s was directed at the eradication of epidemics. Success in this aim, it was believed, would reduce the appalling rate of mortality in towns and make them safer for everyone to live in.

Insanitary living conditions and poor housing were not sudden phenomena of the nineteenth century town. The rural labourer was worse housed than his urban counterpart. Richard Cobden M.P. suggested that rural immigrants sought shelter in the towns *'when the hovels in which they have dwelt fall down around them.'*

Natural decay was sometimes pre-empted by demolition following enclosure. Landlords were prepared to build houses for estate workers but did not wish casual labourers to become a charge upon the parish during periods of unemployment and the demolition of their houses would encourage them to live elsewhere. If the town filled up, as Cobden suggested, with people in search of a home as much as employment, then what they found could not have been encouraging. Although building was proceeding rapidly, the towns' populations were growing faster than the supply of houses. Workers crowded into the once elegant homes of wealthy merchants, or even lived within the works, as Boulton's employees did in his Soho foundry at Birmingham. They doubled up in two-

Nos.1 to 9 John Street and 23 and 25 Parker Street in 1982. The wall on Parker Street was a skin added to the original wall to strengthen it after the internal walls were removed. The doorway of No.25 was hidden. The windows remained. The doorway of No.23 was widened by removing the lintel of 5 John Street and placing it upside down over the door on Parker Street. The original arched doorway is shown in the photograph on page 37. Both photographs show the narrowness of John Street. It was only eighteen feet wide.

roomed cottages and packed into temporary accommodation in fearful lodging houses. Blind-backed houses sprang up along the walls of once pleasant gardens in the towns. Kay and Engels described the result in Manchester's Old Town where Engels discovered *'unqualifiedly the most horrible dwelling which I have ever yet beheld.'*

The change had come about very rapidly in the late eighteenth century. Doctors and clergymen were still vainly trying to assess the population increase as builders worked around the clock and the deficiencies of mediaeval administrative machinery became even more obvious. This inadequacy in Manchester of the Court Leet, and of magistrates, vestries and corporations elsewhere, stimulated a new development in local government, the Improvement Commissioners. Manchester's first Act for 'Cleansing, Lighting and Watching' was obtained in 1792.

The Police Commissioners divided the town into fourteen districts and set about the task of widening and improving streets, making drains and sewers and lighting the town with oil lamps. They laid down building regulations concerning party walls, joists and chimneys, and by 1801 had appointed a paid supervisor of party walls in new buildings. In 1811 another was appointed to survey soughs and drains. John Robertson in 1840 said in the 'Report of the Select Committee on the Health of Towns' that Manchester had no Building Act until 1828, yet from 1792 there were building byelaws and when complaints of contraventions were received the Nuisance Committee could, and did, act.

Further Police Acts were obtained and in 1830 a new Act, and an effective measure in establishing minimum standards for the width of streets, was passed. Unlike the earlier building byelaws, this Act was effective because violations were immediately visible. No new street was to be laid out with a width of less than twenty-four feet. It was too late for John Street; first built upon in 1826-27, it was only eighteen feet across. In future, as soon as one side of a street was built the owner was to pave and drain it. It soon became clear that this was unworkable and the Paving and Soughing Committee began to undertake the work as soon as any part of a street was laid out for building, and then attempted to recover the cost from the owner.

The 1830 building byelaws were strengthened somewhat in 1832, possibly as a result of Kay's investigations, and a further Improvement Act in 1836 gave the Commissioners additional powers *'to prescribe the ground line... of all new buildings.'* Growing awareness that the byelaws were more often than not ignored led to the issuing of Instructions and Regulations for the Superintendent and Inspectors of the Nuisance Department in 1838. These stated that all public nuisances recognised by

Looking up Parker Street in 1898: the corner of 23 Parker Street (right foreground), with No.8 John Street on the right.

either the Police Commissioners or the Court Leet should be reported. Reports were to be made on any new streets laid out with new buildings or old buildings altered or demolished. In fact any violations of the Police Acts, Byelaws for Builders, the General Highway Act or Statutes against Nuisances were to be reported. The requirements were too late to prevent Back Ashley Lane from being built with a width of ten feet and six inches at the wider, and four feet four inches at the narrower end.

Even before the 1792 Police Act, the Court Leet had taken action against 'dangerous cellar holes'; proceedings were numerous after 1788 and more so after 1806. The Police Commissioners too were active on this matter and the Nuisance Committee spent a great deal of time from 1800 onwards dealing with the covering and fencing of cellar entrances. The building byelaws of 1830 and 1832 also concerned themselves with the question. Neither the Court Leet nor the Police Commissioners had powers to prohibit the use of cellars as separate habitations and the three houses built by the Griffin Building Club in 1826-27, and 46 and 48 Back Irk Street, all had separate cellar entrances.

In 1839 the Police Commissioners reported that surveys had been made *'of the whole of the unbuilt part of the town, in order to ascertain the best street levels for buildings; and persons about to build are recommended to apply for the sectional lines at the Paving Offices in the Town Hall.'*

In October 1838 Manchester received its Charter and became a borough. The fight both for and against incorporation had been vigorous. The Charter did not invalidate the Police Acts, so that Police Commissioners continued to act for a further four years, and parliamentary intervention was necessary before the validity of the Charter was accepted by its opponents.

In the 1830s Parliament itself had been intensely active and major reforming legislation had been enacted in spite of the prevailing political philosophy of laissez-faire. The 1840 'Report of the Select Committee on the Health of Towns' was followed in 1841 by three Bills which contained some extremely radical proposals, concerned for the first time with housing rather than sanitation. The most extreme were those proposals to ban back-to-back houses and the use as a dwelling of any cellar which did not have a window, a fireplace and an area. Also to be banned were the building of houses in close alleys, streets of less than thirty feet in width, and house building without prior draining of the site. Finally the Bills called for the provision of drainage for all existing houses.

The Manchester Police Commissioners gave their general approval to the three Bills. They had already taken

The legacy of the early nineteenth century. This street in St Michael's Ward contains bedrooms built over privies and ashpits. The Manchester and Salford Sanitary Association inspectors saw new property being built like this in 1854 by an Alderman, although it contravened local byelaws.

action of their own on some of the evils which the Bills opposed, but two areas of improvement were not welcome to them - those concerned with back-to-back houses and cellar dwellings. Witnesses told the Commons Select Committee that the clause on back-to-backs would raise the cost of the cheapest house from £96 to £119.

'The labouring classes lived in the main in back-to-back houses, covering sixteen superficial yards, for which they paid a rent of two or three shillings, the landlord paying all the rates and making repairs inside and out. Working men with large families took the double house, being enabled to pay the rent by the earnings of their children and the rent they received from lodgers.'

This does not reflect the practice in John Street, where at no time did people living in front and back houses have the same name, although there are cases of families of the same name living in adjacent houses, for example the Woods at 6 and 8 John Street in 1841, and the McCarthys of 8 and 10 Back Ashley Lane from 1859 to 1861.

Witnesses from Liverpool and Leeds agreed with those from Manchester that the proposals were too expensive to be acceptable and the Bills were eventually withdrawn as unworkable. They do give an indication, however, that the housing of the working classes was considered a legitimate concern of Parliament, and these three were the first in a long series of housing Bills, most of which also failed, in the next forty years.

One of the greatest impediments to housing reform was the attitude of middle and upper class Victorians to property and the rights of property owners. Property ownership was seen as a mark of achievement and interference with the rights of private property owners was seen as a dangerous attack on individual liberty.

Enid Gauldie, in 'Cruel Habitations', suggests that this was why the only housing legislation successfully steered through Parliament in the middle decades of the century was incorporated in the Sanitary Acts. Parliament, therefore, left it up to those towns which felt the need to apply for their own local Acts.

In 1844 Manchester's new Borough Council obtained a Police Act, giving the Council wide powers to deal with some of the most urgent social

The steady policy of reconditioning did not solve Manchester's housing problem. Back Ashley Lane, only four feet four inches wide, was reconditioned in 1890, but this house in St Michael's Ward was still inhabited in 1904, the ashbox overflowing and the privy door falling off.

problems, including drunkenness, disorder, domestic sanitation and public health. The most radical clauses concerned the provision of privies and ashpits. All houses built in the future were to have privies and ashpits at the rear, and houses already built were to have privies provided by their owners. This is an example of sanitary legislation affecting housing; what was too expensive to be workable in Normanby's Bill of 1842 was acceptable as a sanitary reform in 1844. As Joseph Heron, the Town Clerk, wrote in 1869, *'the consequence of that legislation has been that in Manchester, since 1844, the building of back-to-back houses...has been illegal.'*

Illegal it may have been, but the Rochdale Road Committee of the Sanitary Association saw two new examples of rows of back-to-backs near John Street in 1854, one still in course of construction. The draft report noted that they were the property of Alderman Pilling, though the fair copy submitted to the City Council omitted this interesting information. They also saw some houses with no privies at all, a situation which should have been remedied after 1844.

The Manchester Corporation Act, also in 1844, gave powers to purchase property in order to open up and ventilate courts. The borough councillors were aware, as were Members of Parliament, that *'the removal of a wall or a shed or a privy, no matter for what object, is an interference with the rights of property'* and Manchester was one of the first authorities to obtain the necessary powers of compulsory acquisition.

The Manchester Corporation Sanitary Act of 1845, as well as making the collection and disposal of night soil a municipal service, also laid down new building byelaws. No three-storey houses were henceforth to be erected in streets of less than ten yards width, nor four-storey houses in streets of less than twelve yards in width.

During the 1840s, three nationwide reports and numerous local reports such as those of the Manchester Statistical Society produced overwhelming evidence of the deplorable sanitary conditions of Britain's towns. The return of King Cholera in 1848-49 convinced many, previously unimpressed by published material, that action was necessary and the first major Sanitary Act of the century became law in 1848.

The Public Health Act was never in force in Manchester, which felt that its own local Acts gave the town wider powers. In the case of the provision of privies and ashpits, Manchester was right. The Public Health Act called for privies and ashpits to be provided *'if there be room without disturbing any building.'* Suspicion of central government was deep and the prospect of supervision by a

VICTORIÆ REGINÆ.

ANNO OCTAVO & NONO

****

Cap. cxli.

An Act to effect Improvements in the Borough of *Manchester* for the Purpose of promoting the Health of the Inhabitants thereof.

[21st *July* 1845.]

LXI. And be it enacted, That it shall be lawful for the Council to appoint and employ or contract with such Number of Persons as they shall from Time to Time think necessary to be Nightmen or Scavengers for emptying and cleansing the Privies within the Borough; and such Nightmen or Scavengers shall, in such Manner as the Council shall appoint, empty and cleanse such of the Privies within the Borough as the Council shall from Time to Time direct, and shall carry away the Soil taken from such Privies to such Place or Places as shall be appointed by the Council for the depositing of the same; and if any such Nightman or Scavenger fail to empty and cleanse any Privy which he shall contract or be employed to empty at the Time or in the Manner prescribed by the Council for that Purpose, or shall deposit the Soil removed from any Privy in any other Place than such as shall be appointed by the Council for that Purpose, he shall for every such Offence forfeit a Sum not exceeding Five Pounds.

LXII. And be it enacted, That every Occupier of a House or other Building within the Borough shall forfeit any Sum not exceeding Five Pounds for every Time he shall prevent any Nightman or Scavenger appointed or employed by or contracting with the Council or his Servants, from emptying and cleansing any Privy which such Nightman or Scavenger shall have been directed by the Council to empty and cleanse.

Paragraphs from Manchester Corporation's 1845 Sanitary Act relating to the establishment of a night soil collection service.

Central Board of Health was most unwelcome in Manchester. During the next generation Manchester was left to get on with its own sanitary reform and from that time onwards, central government, however slowly, began to pull ahead of Manchester. Legislation empowered towns and cities to act on housing, but it was 1890 before opinion in Manchester came into line with the new laws.

The most radical housing Act of the century was steered through Parliament in 1851 by Lord Shaftesbury. The Lodging Houses Act was the first to be specifically concerned with the housing of working class people. Council house building and the assumption of state responsibility for the housing of the poor were made possible by Shaftesbury's Act and the intention was to provide more than lodging houses for single persons; families were to be catered for. It was too radical to escape serious amendment and one such clause laid down that ratepayers who objected to the use of their money for the housing of working class people could delay the implementation until after a local election. This provision ensured that the Act would become a dead letter. Another amendment ensured that sexes would be segregated.

In 1883 Lord Shaftesbury said that only Huddersfield had used the Act as he had meant it to be used. Huddersfield's model lodging house was opened in 1854. In most towns, including Manchester, the building of such lodging houses was left to philanthropists who hoped to stimulate speculative builders to follow their example. The 1885 Housing of the Working Classes Act made it clear that lodging houses were *'deemed to include separate houses or cottages... whether containing one or several tenements.'*

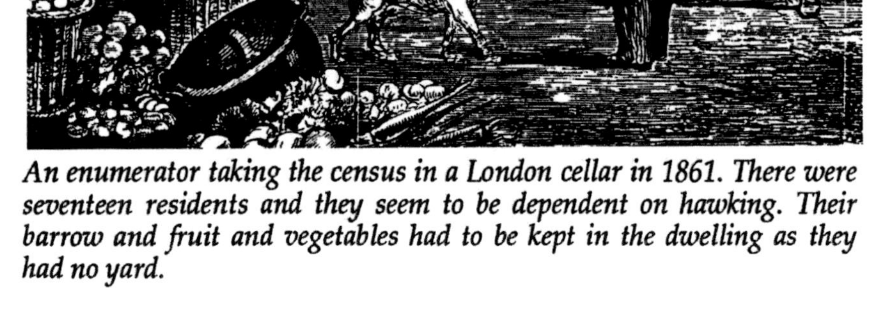

An enumerator taking the census in a London cellar in 1861. There were seventeen residents and they seem to be dependent on hawking. Their barrow and fruit and vegetables had to be kept in the dwelling as they had no yard.

Sanitary legislation continued to affect housing but most of the Acts of the 1850s and 1860s had the effect of intensifying the misery of those who lived in inadequate accommodation. One example is the Nuisances Removal Act of 1855, which conveyed the power and stressed the duty of local authorities to order the closing of houses where the nuisance was such *'as to render the house unfit for human habitation.'* This was the first recognition in law that there could be a dwelling too awful for a person to live in and that there was some standard below which housing conditions should not fall.

Medical Officers of Health, however, were already aware, as legislators and the general public were not until the 1880s, that the closure of one dwelling as 'unfit' promptly rendered others unfit which may not have been before, as those displaced crowded into the already overcrowded buildings which remained.

The steady pressure of the Manchester and Salford Sanitary Association, which in the absence of a Medical Officer of Health fulfilled some of his functions, led to some Improvement Bills which failed through the opposition of pressure groups and vested interests. A river pollution Bill was opposed by the canal companies and the Mersey and Irwell Navigation Company. The Manchester Corporation New Streets Act of 1853 was ineffective in closing down cellar dwellings because of strenuous opposition from the hastily formed House Owners' Guardian Association. In the next six years only 176 cellars were closed.

The late 1860s brought about a

change in Manchester. The annual meeting of the Social Sciences Congress, which in 1866 was devoted to housing, met here. Criticism was expressed of the host city and a report recommended *'a complete remodelling of the Sanitary Department of the Corporation and the appointment of a responsible Medical Officer of Health.'*

The building byelaws for which powers had been obtained in 1865 were adopted in 1867, and a Medical Officer of Health was appointed in 1868. The Manchester Waterworks Improvement Act of 1867 proved to be a major weapon in John Leigh's war on Manchester's deplorably high mortality rate. Throughout most of the century Manchester had been in the top three of the nation's unhealthiest towns.

It was clear to anyone that a sufficient supply of decent and sanitary houses would bring down the mortality rates, yet Leigh, a doctor active in the town for over thirty years, was aware that Manchester had a peculiar difficulty in providing decent working class housing. The town was completely built up and land prices in consequence were exceedingly high. Demolition of cheaply rented housing released land which was eagerly snapped up by industry or commerce at a price which would have made the replacement of reasonably rented housing quite impossible. The working classes had to be shifted to the edges or beyond the boundaries of the city, where there was still land available at lower prices. Without cheap transport, however, working people could not afford to move, and people in casual employment, porters and general labourers of the sort who lived in John Street, had to be housed near their work.

Although Leigh realised the problems, he was a typical product of his age. He believed that private enterprise should and would provide where there was a clear need. If people needed houses, then houses would appear. He believed, as did so many housing reformers, that if the artisans and those in regular employment obtained better houses, then those they vacated would become available for the people one grade below on the social scale, and so on down to the bottom. It was very perplexing and disappointing to those who gave the housing problem any serious thought when this did not happen.

Leigh therefore set his face firmly against demolition. Demolition would make things worse. His answer was reconditioning, that is, bringing the existing housing stock up to standard at the owners' expense, not the ratepayers'. In taking this line Leigh actually had a somewhat better answer than the people who framed the major housing legislation of the 1860s and 1870s, Torrens and Cross.

The Torrens and Cross Acts of 1868 and 1874 were slum-clearance Acts, Torrens' for individual properties and Cross's for whole areas. Leigh and other Medical Officers already realised that slum clearance did not rehouse those rendered homeless. Leigh worked under the Local Act of 1867, which allowed two inspectors or himself to close a house which was unfit, without compensation, at a month's notice. It was up to the owner to make the next move. If he wished the property to continue as a dwelling, he had to satisfy the Medical Officer. If he wished to re-let it for other purposes, that was up to him, as long as it conformed to the relevant byelaws. Both Leigh's successors, far more radical than he, continued this policy. By 1904 over 6,000 houses, mostly back-to-backs, had been closed, but less than 3,000 were built.

Leigh also closed down 2,400 cellar dwellings between 1868 and 1872, including the five at John Street, and by 1874 only 108 remained. Manchester was no longer, as he had said in 1869, *'a city of cave dwellers.'* The

Nos.4 and 6 Back Ashley Lane in 1982. The extension was added some time between 1890 and 1911 after reconditioning and contained two water closets. These were the only water closets in John Street's history.

replacement of about 40,000 insanitary midden privies with pail privies took him about ten years. Leigh again was being practical. No-one could deny that water closets were the most sanitary way of disposing of 'excrementitious matter' but Sir Joseph Heron, in giving evidence before the Sanitary Commission in 1871, argued that there was not enough water for water closets, that sewage irrigation on the land was impossible for Manchester and that it would cost £1,000,000 to take it out to sea. It was not until 1876 that the Rivers Committee received a report from its officials recommending the construction of intercept sewers and a treatment works at Davyhulme. Manchester had to wait for boundary changes to enlarge the city and the additional income from the rates and agreement with neighbouring authorities before this report could be acted upon.

Leigh's pragmatic approach was also evident in his attitude to back-to-back housing. The miasmic theory of disease was the main reason for the preoccupation of sanitary reformers with ventilation. By their very construction the back-to-back houses of the nineteenth century could not obtain a through draught. Part of Leigh's campaign of reconditioning had been to have the back-to-backs knocked into 'through houses' and given back yards. The problem was enormous and by the time Leigh retired in 1888 there were still 10,000 in Manchester.

A lodging house in Angel Street in 1904.

Medical Officers everywhere were beginning to draw attention to the fact that *'the rate of mortality from all causes is higher among the dwellers in back-to-back houses than among the same classes in "through" houses.'*

Drs Tatham and Niven took on this problem and gave it greater priority. By 1900 half of the back-to-backs had gone and less than 100 remained in 1913. Leigh had, of course, seen that even reconditioning of back-to-backs did not solve the housing problem. Five families had to find other accommodation when Back Ashley Lane was knocked through into John Street in 1891. Niven commented that *'piecemeal operations of the Unhealthy Dwellings Sub-Committee resulted in only a limited local displacement...in order to diminish the inconvenience sustained by the closing of houses care was taken to distribute the committee's operations so that the distress should be distributed as widely as possible at any given time,'* which was implicit recognition that legislation so far was essentially negative in spirit.

Slowly, Manchester and the country were groping their way towards a more constructive approach. Standards for new buildings were being improved; Manchester's first building byelaws for over twenty years made a yard of at least 70 feet square compulsory for each house. At the same time Parliament was making money available through the Public Works Loans Commissioners for the erection of 'Labourers' Dwellings' in populous towns. The money was borrowed almost exclusively by dwelling companies, Liverpool being the only corporation to take advantage of it to build St Martin's Cottages in 1868.

Parliament still believed that private enterprise or philanthropy would rehouse those made homeless through clearances under the Torrens and Cross Acts, and that these were the proper channels through which rehousing ought to be effected. Local authorities clearly shared the opinion of Parliament, since they did not avail themselves of the opportunities which they had been given to rehouse the displaced. Leigh himself suggested that the activities of the housing and social reformer Octavia Hill and the dwellings associations might be emulated but 'five per cent philanthropy' attracted virtually no investors in Manchester. Only two attempts at philanthropic block housing seem to have been made in Manchester; one of them at Holt Town, by the Manchester and Salford Workmen's Dwellings Company, and the other in Ancoats. This was a conversion, in 1892, of a cotton mill into 141 tenements and was an employer's scheme.

Although Manchester opposed the passage of the Cross Act in 1875, Leigh admitted that the 'exigencies of commerce', which had done so much to clear the slums of Manchester, had not effected the improvements he had hoped for and that the commercial districts still contained the worst housing. Even the recently erected dwellings near the city boundary, to which he had encouraged the working classes to migrate by the demolition or reconditioning of their old houses, *'commence where the old houses leave off, and are rotten from the start.'*

Victoria Square Dwellings, Oldham Road, in 1914. (See page 46)

However, he recognised that the cost of buying up the largest area in need of improvement would be over £1,000,000 and so he did not recommend it. Reconditioning under the Local Acts of 1867 continued. The Griffin houses were closed in 1888, the back-to-backs knocked through in 1891 and John Street condemned in 1903.

In 1885 the Royal Commission on the Housing of the Working Classes had published its report. The Commission had been set up to examine the working of the Housing Acts of 1868 and 1875. Its conclusion, both shocking and disappointing, was that laissez-faire, market forces and philanthropy had failed to provide sufficient or adequate housing for working class people; that demolitions under the Torrens and Cross Acts, by railway companies and by commerce had considerably reduced the number of houses available to the poor and had pushed up the rents of those that remained. This in turn had increased overcrowding. Housing conditions for that section of the population which Cobden called the 'residuum' were worse than they had ever been. The housing associations and local authorities which had tried to help them had not housed those who were in most need.

The first commandment of the managers and directors of model dwellings was that the rent - and Octavia Hill, for example, set her rents realistically, as low as 2/- per week - must be paid regularly. In slum houses neighbours could have a 'whip round' to help, the landlord could be fobbed off for a week or two, or there was always the 'moonlight flit' when arrears became too high. Arrears were not permitted in model dwellings and thus the out-workers, the casual labourers and porters could not hope to live in housing association or corporation property where it existed. The concluding findings were that sanitary improvements had not greatly affected the mortality rate and that overcrowding caused by poverty was the real cause of slums, not the 'filthy and dissolute' habits of the slum dwellers.

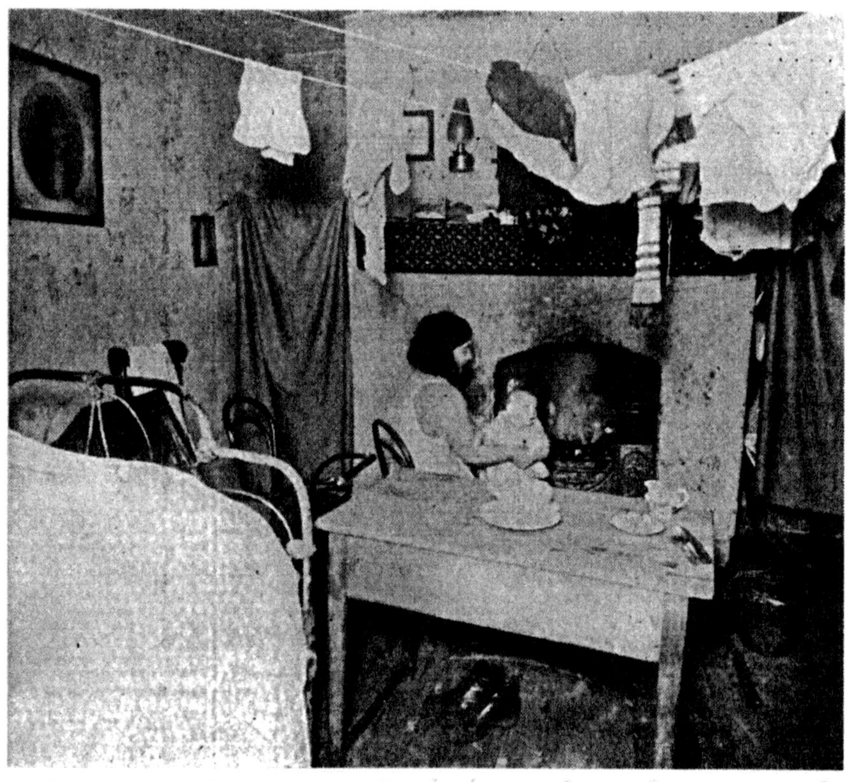

A Manchester slum in 1932. The single-room home of a young couple and their two children in an Ancoats lodging house.

Andrew Mearns had already aroused middle class consciousness to the true state of the poor with his 'Bitter Cry of Outcast London' in 1883, and in the 'Pall Mall Gazette' in 1885 P D Hyndman had claimed that 25% of Londoners were living in abject poverty. In Manchester John Leigh, nearing the end of his career, had reached the conclusion that the provision of houses at a rent people could afford to pay was no more Socialism, as some had claimed, than the provision of roads and drains, and if *'helping the poor in this way, doing for them what they cannot do for themselves, or aiding them to do what they cannot accomplish alone, be Socialism or Communism, the more we have of it, the better, when wisely and judiciously administered.'*

Demolition in Style Street, corner of Irk Street, in 1939.

In spite of the final and characteristic qualification this, from John Leigh, was revolutionary. At the national level, too, a constructive approach to housing had gained an important new convert in Lord Salisbury, the leader of the Conservative party, who introduced the new Housing of the Working Classes Act to the Lords.

Two Housing Acts followed the Report of the Royal Commission, the first in 1885 and the second, consolidating Act, in 1890. There was very little that was new in either of them, since they empowered local authorities to use public money to build dwellings for the working classes, which had been legally possible since 1851. Victoria Square was erected under the 'Manchester Labourers' Dwellings Scheme, 1890' in Oldham Road Clearance Area No.2 and had its first tenants in 1894.

John Street's story serves to illuminate the housing activities and policies of the township, the borough and the city of Manchester during the period of rapid growth and equally rapid decay. Built before effective building controls, in a street too narrow to meet the requirements even of the Police Act of 1830, the houses, back-to-back with cellar dwellings, sheltered a minute fraction of the teeming multitudes which poured into Manchester in the first half of the nineteenth century. The rest of the century was needed to improve and finally to close them.

During this time, Manchester had taken the lead in setting the example to the rest of the country; a determined effort was made to prevent the building of new slums and to eliminate the worst aspects of those it already had. After this flying start Manchester slipped back. There was no Medical Officer of Health as there had been in Liverpool since 1846, nor a determined body of housing reformers in Parliament, as Scotland had. Manchester's exclusion from the General Board of Health after 1848 and the delay in appointing a Medical Officer are symptomatic of a lack of urgency, general throughout the country. John Leigh, cautious and steady, may have been practical in his approach, but reconditioning did not solve Manchester's housing problem. Leigh's failure was not unique, however, and those towns which attempted to tackle the problem with ratepayers' money, like Liverpool or Dundee, were no more successful. London left it to the housing associations to find the answers, and they too failed. What was necessary was a knowledge of the true causes of slums (obscured by the sanitary idea for most of the century) and the political will to tackle them. When, during the mid 1880s, John Leigh, Lord Salisbury and Joseph Chamberlain found themselves in agreement over the need for state and municipal action, then public opinion could not be far behind. By 1890 Manchester and the country were ready to do what Shaftesbury's Act had made possible in 1851, and local authorities at last took upon themselves the responsibility for housing the working classes.

The chance survival of the John Street properties led to this book. Curiosity about their history could not be satisfied by the general accounts of Russell and Lady Simon; only research could tell their story. The research revealed that the joiner's shop in Collyhurst was a perfect example of the thousands of slums in nineteenth century Manchester.

St Michael's Churchyard, Ashley Lane and Charter Street Ragged School in 1972. Beyond the railway line are the rooftops of John Street (arrowed) and Ashley Lane Sunday School.